Wanna see something funny?

If you do, good luck. Humor in today's cinema is in an uncertain state. On one hand, sophisticated comedy has reached such a pretentious level that only the most contemplative navel-gazers can scarcely manage a chuckle. On the other, humor for the masses seems to become more obsessed with toilet functions with each passing year. (Apologies to those who prefer the less then subtle shadings of bathroom humor. If that's you, don't forget to flush!) One should never overanalyze the comic instinct, of course, lest we lose the intuitive spark that awakens the child within us. Still, it seems that there must be a happy medium, where the belly laughs are more than just a passing and quickly forgotten diversion.

So what's a movie lover to do?

The answer lies, as it often does, in the past. For there, obscured by the decades and confined to a screen that has no voice, is Hollywood's perfect gift to lovers of humor everywhere—the magic and mirth of silent comedy. Silent comedy, as wild as a drunken chorus girl and as rude as a whoopee cushion, is just the thing to cure those gas-prices-too-high, job-prospects-too-low living-in-the-21st-century blues.

While the uninformed may be tempted to write off cinema from the pre-sound era as unworthy of viewing today, fans of silent comedy know better. Far from being merely a technical limitation, the absence of sound created a stylized world that heightened the laugh potential to a fever pitch. In addition, the typical two-reeler of this era was created in a team environment, with plot lines improvised and gags enhanced on the spot. This wonderful adlibbed quality was lost when the rigid dictates of sound came along, never to be recaptured again. Cinema may have made a quantum leap when talking film became the accepted norm, but the world of film comedy has never been the same since.

The following list of recommended silent comedy viewing is based solely on the personal tastes of this writer. The usual suspects are here, along with some admittedly lesser but still worthy choices that are often overlooked. Although

American Wedding, starring Jason Biggs (top), made liberal use of bathroom humor for laughs while Laurel and Hardy (bottom) epitomize the magic and mirth of silent comedy.

the list is subjective, readers will hopefully find these choices to be informed and balanced. And along with the officially sanctioned goal of deepening an appreciation for the history of the cinema (hey, stop that yawning!), it is my hope that people will discover something funny along the way—something that will both delight the mind and tickle the soul.

Let the laughter begin!

Charlie Chaplin was once universally revered as one of the icons of American cinema. In recent decades, revisionists have succeeded in taking some of the luster off his legend. Questions over his political allegiances have proven to be off-putting to some, while others find his sentimental touches far too cloying for modern tastes. (Conversely, there is also a subset of modern viewers who find his knockabout treatment of authority figures to be unacceptably violent!) Consistent with the build 'em up, knock 'em down mentality of the modern era,

poor Charlie, it would seem, can no longer catch a break.

But for lovers of film comedy, none of the above should matter. Chaplin's status as a giant of the pre-sound era remains secure, buttressed by a body of work that impresses us still, nearly a century later. While much of the humor in the age of Keystone and Sennett is a puzzle to us today, Chaplin's films still make a connection, demonstrating that laughter does indeed have a universal appeal.

Early film comedy was largely a mechanical affair, with each film crammed to the brim with predictable gags and improbable situations. Chaplin helped change all this. His character of the Tramp, whose elfin charm could manifest itself in delightfully unexpected ways, became a figure of wish fulfillment for filmgoers of the silent years. Whether pulling the rug out from under the feet of bullying adversaries or magically mastering such elaborate skills as skating and tightrope walking, Charlie bridged the gap between fantasy and reality, with one foot firmly in each camp. Humor was thus developed from character as often as it was derived from situation, an approach that the audience of the late 1910s (and, even more remarkably, the cinema fans of today) responded to with unconditional approval. Such innovative touches add much to early Chaplin classics like *The Rink, Easy Street* and *One A.M.*, which are required viewing for any student of early cinema.

Chaplin is also celebrated for overlapping the boundaries of comedy into the areas of tragedy and pathos. A dicey proposal for some, this approach nonetheless brought new and deeper resonance to his films. As early as 1915's *The Tramp*, Charlie was experimenting with ways to incorporate both smiles and sympathy into his popular two-reelers. In his later features like *The Kid* and *City Lights*, this formula was worked to heart-rending perfection. As a consequence, Chaplin's full-length films reveal more substance than the works of other comedians, allowing him to reach an audience that traditionally did not go for the comical stuff.

More importantly, Chaplin was just plain funny. With pinpoint timing developed from

Charlie Chaplin in *The Gold Rush*

Mad About Movies
Number 4

Editors
Gary J. Svehla
Susan Svehla

Managing Editor
Richard J. Svehla

Copy Editor
Linda J. Walter

Graphic Design Interior
Susan Svehla

Cover Design/Title Page Design
Susan Svehla

Contributing Writers
Mark Clark, Todd M. Gault, Jeff Miller
Carl Schultz, Gary J. Svehla, Steven Thornton

Acknowledgments
Photofest/Buddy Weiss

Publisher
Midnight Marquee Press

Mad About Movies
Number 4
Copyright 2004 © by Gary J. Svehla
  Published twice yearly by Midnight Marquee Press at $17 per year. Printed by Boyd Printing, Albany, NY.
  Return postage must accompany articles and art, if the owner wants them returned. No responsibility is taken for unsolicited material. Editorial views expressed by our contributors are not necessarily those of the publisher. Nothing may be reproduced in any media without written permission of the publisher. Send submissions of articles, letters and art to Gary J. Svehla, 9721 Britinay Lane, Baltimore, MD 21234; web site: http://www.midmar.com; e-mail: mmarquee@aol.com
  Letters of comment addressed to Mad About Movies or Gary or Susan Svehla will be considered for publication unless the writer requests otherwise. Subscription rates: $10 per single copy or $17 per year (shipped U.S. Media Mail). Subscription copies are mailed in sturdy cardboard mailers and will arrive in excellent condition; support MidMar by becoming a direct-mail subscriber. Foreign orders are $39 (U.S.) for a two-issue subscription.

TABLE OF CONTENTS

3 **The Roar of the Crowd**
   Letters

4 **The Laughter of Silents**
   by Steven Thornton

18 **Lionel Atwill's Serial Adventures**
   by Todd M. Gault

28 **Alfred Hitchcock's** *Saboteur*
   by Mark Clark

35 **Ronald Reagan and** *Casablanca*: **Debunking the Myth**
   by Carl Schultz

38 **Robert Lees (1912-2004) A Tribute**
   by Jeff Miller

41 **The DVDs are Afoot**
   The Sherlock Holmes Collection
   by Gary J. Svehla

53 **Mad About Movies DVD Reviews**
   by Gary J. Svehla

Welcome to *Mad About Movies* #4. As usual we're late getting the mag out, but we hope it will have been worth the wait.

With the New Year rapidly approaching, we will soon be bombarded with multiple film award shows, where Hollywood indulges in endless self-congratulation while once again proving they have no idea what will play in Peoria. The teenage CEOs running the film industry persistently underestimate the intelligence of their mainstream audience. Film lovers looking for light-hearted escapist entertainment are forced to choose either gross-out teenage comedies filled with bathroom humor and juvenile sex jokes, or glorified independents, darlings of critics and art houses everywhere. Not your cup of tea? Ours either. We never did see what that *Something About Mary* was. So scratch most teenage fare. As for the independents, those angst ridden, usually depressing films are (mis)labeled comedies if they manage to generate one measly chuckle. *Hedwig and the Angry Inch* (a gay Berlin man falls in love with a U.S. sergeant, who will only take him back to the States if he has a sex change. The doctors botch the job and leave an inch (hence the title). The sergeant abandons Hedwig in a Kansas trailer park. Yes, this movie was a laugh a minute. *USA Today* gave *Hedwig* 3 1/2 stars! *Lost in Translation* won a slew of awards including the Golden Globe for Best Musical or Comedy. I'm not sure if I watched the movie or my watch more. I thought this film would never end—and as for calling it a comedy, I don't think so.

What is the film lover, who is looking for a little happily mindless escapism, to do? Ignore the smirks of pretentious film snobs and turn on the Cartoon Network, the Disney Channel or Nickelodeon. *The Incredibles, Finding Nemo, Shrek, Monsters, Inc., Holes, Tarzan, Toy Story, Pirates of the Caribbean,* even *George of the Jungle* provided harmless entertainment galore, dazzling colors and sparking dialogue. Even television cartoons provide hours of enjoyment because the writers write to entertain themselves as well as their young audience. *Sponge Bob Square Pants* offered an episode filmed as one of those deadly instructional 16mm films we were forced to watch in grade school. *Animaniacs* is filled with obscure classic film jokes and references as the Warner Brothers (Yakko [Groucho Marx reborn], Wakko [without a doubt Ringo Starr]) and their sister Dot share adventures on the Warner Bros. lot with Slappy the Squirrel (a cranky former classic cartoon star, who takes care of her nephew Skippy), Pinky and the Brain (who is modeled after Orson Welles) and Bobby, Pesto and Squit, the pigeon goodfeathers who adore Martin Scorsese and sound a lot like Jack Nicholson and Joe Pesci. There is even a website listing all the movie in-jokes on *Animaniacs* (www.geocities.com/Hollywood/Lot/2636/crg/). Also check out *Jimmy Neutron, The Fairly Oddparents, Hey Arnold, Dexter's Laboratory, Johnny Bravo, Evil Con Carne* (a mad scientist who sounds like Ricardo Montalban has his brain and stomach implanted into a stupid bear, tries to take over the world as his female mad doctor tries to induce him to fall in love with her, while his evil general keeps trying to destroy him…well just watch it), *Duck Dodgers, The Grim Adventures of Billy and Mandy* (way bizarre)—the list could go on and on, but take my word for it, when you're in the mood for some zany but intelligent laughs, pretend you're a kid again and watch some cartoons.

And we need all the laughs we can get after the past year. Hollywood's lights grew a little dimmer in 2004 with the deaths of Bob Keeshan, Ann Miller, Francis Dee, Peter Ustinov, Alan King, Anna Lee, Tony Randall, Marlon Brando, composer Jerry Goldsmith, Virginia Grey, Fay Wray, composer Elmer Bernstein, Janet Leigh, Howard Keel, Ed Kemmer (star of *Space Patrol* and a guest at one of our FANEX film conventions, as were Janet Leigh and Acquanetta, who also passed away this year).

We also lost one of our writers and good friend John E. Parnum. John contributed to *Midnight Marquee* for over 20 years. He was also one of FANEX's most dedicated supporters and he attended every convention from the first to FANEX 17, our last show, which was held in 2003. Sadly, I also lost my mother this year after an extremely painful illness she had had for the past two years. She came to Baltimore every year from her home in Johnstown to help us run FANEX. She never understood our movie obsession and rarely knew who any of the guests were, but she helped us just the same. Our good friend Polly says when she hits the lottery she's going to give us the money to do FANEX: The Director's Cut. I just don't think it would be the same. So many of the old stars, who really enjoyed meeting the fans and were not just faking it to make a buck, are gone. And with the state of the world people would rather just stay home and watch those old gems when Hollywood knew the meaning of "Shakin' the Blues Away" (one of Ann Miller's greatest musical numbers, which was from *Easter Parade*).

Mom's favorite part of our magazine was Gary's editorials, so this one is dedicated to Aurelia Miller, who will always be in our memories.
Susan Svehla

Top to bottom: Ann Miller, Fay Wray, Kathryn Grayson and Howard Keel from *Showboat*, John Parnum and Tom Johnson pose at FANEX and Aurelia Miller helps at FANEX 6 registration.

Dear Susan and Gary:

Your issue #2 of *Mad About Movies* is my introduction to this new magazine from Midnight Marquee Press, Inc. so I want to start with my congratulations and best wishes for its success.

I'm disappointed to know that the picture on which John Wayne had the most fun was *Hartari* because it was filmed in Africa. I would have loved him to say *The Three Musketeers* (the Mascot serial) with its equally exotic settings on the screen, although undoubtedly that was shot in the wilds of California's deserts. I particularly liked the article on Perry Mason, whom today's audiences only think of as Raymond Burr on television. I wish Clair Schulz would now do a similar survey on Philo Vance, although a Vance filmography would involve many more titles, a greater number of actors playing S.S. Van Dine's private investigator and even extend to England where Wilfrid Hyde White played Philo Vance in a British thriller made by Paramount called *The Scarab Murder Case*.

I've always admired Jim Coughlin's research on "forgotten faces" and this time he caught me out as I had never heard the name Wirley Birch before. I certainly share Gary Svehla's enthusiasm about the newly released DVDs of the Doctor Mabuse series. I came across the good (?) doctor for the first time when I was ten years old and my grandmother took me to see Lang's 1931 *Testament of Dr. Mabuse*, the first and only movie that frightened me out of my wits while I was watching it and gave me nightmares for a week afterwards, something for which my mother never forgave my grandmother! It is only fitting that Fritz Lang's last hurrah was a new take on Doctor Mabuse and we owe a debt of gratitude to David Kalat for bringing it back in such fine and original form on DVD. Unfortunately the six Mabuse films subsequently produced by Artur Brauner are vastly inferior and are more in the style of the German Edgar Wallace action thrillers that were so popular at the same time than attempting to recapture the essence of the great Mabuse pictures from the 1920s and 1930s.

An interesting point about the Mickey Spillane film *The Girl Hunters* is that, despite its American stars, setting and director, it was actually a British film. Charles Reynolds, its English executive producer, intended it to be the first of a series if it had been more successful at the box office.

To return, for a moment, to Doctor Mabuse, readers will be pleased to know that actor Wolfgang Preiss, who played the Mabuse role so brilliantly in *Thousand Eyes of Dr. Mabuse* and Artur Brauner's subsequent series, is still alive and well and living in Germany. Last year he celebrated his 90th birthday and he sent me a beautiful color photograph of himself that he autographed in which he doesn't look a day older than when he was bent on the destruction of law and order!

Richard Gordon

Dear Susan and Gary:

Your aptly titled *Mad About Movies* is a ripsnorter of a magazine as one would say here in Australia. I adore the monster movies from the past, but it's quite refreshing to see you covering a wide variety of genres from Westerns, crime, comedy to even musicals. However, I'd like to request specifically the following series films be covered in insightful articles: Jungle Jim, Bomba the Jungle Boy, The Bowery Boys, Ma and Pa Kettle, The Falcon, The Shadow, The Whistler, Crime Doctor, etc. I suspect there my be enough titles for some of your excellent wordsmiths to even properly tackle it in book format.

I'm also eagerly anticipating an in-depth analysis of the film collaborations of that sinister pair, Sydney Greenstreet and Peter Lorre.

I hope you keep my suggestions in mind for future issues. In the meantime keep up the great work, magazines and books included.

Carmelo Bazzano

Dear Susan and Gary:

MAM #3 was great as you got into one of my top-10 films, *The Quiet Man*, and the Laurel and Hardy silents, so far superior to their sound films. Hope you can find someone to write about *Yoyimbo* (1961), such a great film with an excellent acting job by Toshiro Mifume, at least to my eyes.

Alan Grossman

Dear Susan and Gary:

All good things are worth waiting for!

My favorite article in the second issue of *MAM* was *Perry Mason in the Movies*. I have always had a fascination toward the literary character and as he was depicted on TV and in the movies.

I am also a fan of British comedian Benny Hill and heard he made a few movies. I would very much love to read an in-depth article on his feature films. Also, I would love to read any articles on any unusual British comedians.

Lawrence Loftin

Dear Susan and Gary:

I loved your second issue of *Mad About Movies*, and especially enjoyed the indepth analyses on the Perry Mason movie series and the Kay Keyser movies. I have all those titles on video except *My Favorite Spy*.

Elwin F. Hartwig

his tutelage in the English music hall and a natural gift for mimicry, Charlie was a springboard of comic invention. Surviving outtakes from his films reveal discarded gags with innumerable variations, all equally pleasing to the eye. Most comics would have given their funny bone to conceive such an embarrassment of comic wealth. And even when executing gags that originated elsewhere, such as the celebrated "dance of the rolls" in *The Gold Rush*, Chaplin's execution was so adroit that his creative stamp left a permanent mark. Although the "borrowing" of routines was common in the silent and early sound era, few comedians would ever dare to revisit such signature gags as this again.

What Charlie Chaplin was the to heart, Buster Keaton (shown here with Big Joe Roberts in *Neighbors*) was to the mind.

Chaplin's films have been widely available since the early days of film collecting, a testament to both his undying popularity and to the public domain status of much of his work. This proliferation of Chaplin material continues to the present day, with his best material readily available on DVD. Image Entertainment has released a seven-disc compilation of the Essanay and Mutual shorts that were restored to near pristine condition, an essential purchase for true connoisseurs of movie comedy. Warner Home Video, in cooperation with the Chaplin estate, has also made available the entire run of Chaplin features on DVD, complete with copious audio and visual supplements. Various other bargain basement releases are also available for those looking to save a buck. But let the buyer beware—the genius of Charlie Chaplin demands the visual perfection that only a quality DVD release can deliver.

What Charlie Chaplin was to the heart, Buster Keaton was to the mind. Born into a barnstorming, show-biz family, Buster quickly became part of the act, and his life's journey as an entertainer was underway. Although he lagged in popularity behind Chaplin, audiences of the 1920s appreciated Keaton for his unique and quirky comic vision. History has since confirmed this judgment and now places him at the very peak of the silent film pantheon.

Keaton's efforts to master the challenges of the physical world continue to delight even today's audiences. Like a mechanical engineer from Mars, he would approach the most mundane problems and devise the damnedest solutions to them. Even more amazing was the fact that, when seen through his admittedly skewed vision, his solutions seemed not unreasonable at all. Augmenting this was Buster's natural skill as an acrobat, a talent gleaned from his years in his family's knockabout stage shows. Episodes like the famous teeter-totter, tug-of-war scene from 1922's *Cops* combined athletic prowess with an absurd visual touch that few comics could match.

Just as essential to the Keaton style was an existential quality that, in an unassuming

Buster Keaton in *The General*

production as an independent filmmaker. (A bonus disc also captures rare film and television appearances from the latter decades of his life.) Image Entertainment has also released a DVD pairing of two of his most satisfying features, *The General* and *Steamboat Bill Jr*. Buster Keaton may have appeared eternally forlorn onscreen, but in the history of silent cinema, he is a winner all the way.

way, bordered on the profound. Whether trapped in a sinking vessel in *The Boat* or caught in front of an errant cannon in *The General*, Buster often found himself standing in the pathway of certain disaster. Then, when all seemed lost, life would suddenly and unexpectedly provide a way to safety. A cosmic commentary on the condition of man? Perhaps, but in any case the comic possibilities of this "surrender and be saved" philosophy provide further evidence of Keaton's cerebral approach to screen comedy.

Buster's skill as a filmmaker should also be acknowledged. Unlike many silent comics, who clung to the proscenium-based look of the stage, Keaton quickly mastered the art of camera placement and film editing, giving his films a pace and an economy that stands toe to toe with the best directors of the 1920s. Camera trickery was often employed as an integral part of the storyline. Seeing Buster multiple-exposed as an entire orchestra in *The Playhouse* or watching him join the action of an onscreen movie in *Sherlock Jr.*, one can only marvel at his limitless bag of cinematic tricks.

Those who want to experience this gifted comedian firsthand need look no further than Kino's exhaustive DVD collection, *The Art of Buster Keaton*. This 10-disc (!) set chronicles his career from the early shorts to his final

Most comedians of the silent screen adopted an outlandish persona as their identifying trademark. A notable exception was Harold Lloyd. The most "normal" of the silent comics, Lloyd crafted a screen identify that reflected the hopes and dreams of the Roaring Twenties—a decent but humble soul who through hard work, perseverance and dumb luck overcame countless obstacles to find success and happiness, all in time for the closing reel.

Lloyd spent many years in the training ground of two-reelers before striking gold in the early 1920s. The change was ushered in when Harold added a pair of spectacles to his screen attire; this new look conveyed character nuances and suggested comedic possibilities that had previously been untapped. He explored these possibilities in a series of features extending into the sound era, creating a body of work that holds up superbly today. While never regarded as a genius on the level of Chaplin or Keaton, Lloyd was a master of comedic acting and intuitively understood what made an audience laugh.

Harold Lloyd's first claim to fame was the "thrill" comedy. Inspired when he saw a daredevil scale the exterior of a tall building, Lloyd envisioned the use of danger to increase the tension and thus heighten the laugh quotient of his films. A series of comedies then followed in which his character was placed in a variety of precarious circumstances, often involving the upper reaches of an unfinished skyscraper. *Safety Last* epitomized this approach; the film's image of Lloyd dangling from the hands of a clock some 20 stories above street level remains one of the iconic images of silent cinema. Filmed from an elevation that towered above the surrounding locale, the scene has a heart-stopping veracity that even modern CGI cannot duplicate.

Just as important to Lloyd's style was the human touch that set him apart from other comics. In films like *The Freshman* and *The Kid Brother*, Lloyd portrayed well-meaning but ineffectual characters who longed to prove themselves to the world. The element of romance in his stories was far more than just the window dressing needed to woo female viewers—it became the very catalyst that triggered his metamorphosis into a man of self-determination. Decisive action followed, leading to a climax in which challenges were met head on and self-respect was finally attained. Harold's films, consequently, call to mind a Horatio Alger story that inspires his audiences in addition to making them smile. (As an aside, Lloyd experienced a real-life tragedy during the making of one of his early films when a prop bomb blew away the thumb and forefinger of his right hand. Refusing to quit, he used a flesh-colored glove to hide the deformity and began making movies anew, a true-life example of the "can do" spirit that his films embodied.)

From a technical perspective, Harold Lloyd is remembered for one of Hollywood's most practical innovations—previewing a film before a live audience. Through the use of this device, he was able to obtain direct feedback from his

Harold Lloyd strikes a comic pose in *Speedy*.

fan base, allowing him to perfect gags and tweak plot points to improve a film's overall impact. Sequences like the delirious chase scenes at the climax of *Girl Shy* and *Speedy* benefit greatly from this approach, their narratives accelerated to a nail-biting pace that is nearly unbearable. Even today, when action is the buzzword used to

Harold Lloyd in his most famous scene in *Safety Last*

sell Hollywood movies, filmmakers could take a cue from the mathematically precise editing employed by Harold Lloyd.

The availability of Lloyd's work has always been an issue for fans of early cinema. An astute businessman, Harold retained the rights to his most successful features, inadvertently keeping them out of the hands of film collectors who jumpstarted the renewed appreciation of silent comedy in the 1960s and '70s. The Lloyd estate has long promised a major DVD release of his film catalog, but thus far has delivered nothing. As a step in the right direction, Kino, in cooperation with Europe's Lobster Films (yes, you got the name right), is making available several of Lloyd's early shorts and the feature film *Grandma's Boy* on a soon-to-be-released DVD set, *The Harold Lloyd Collection*. Let's hope that more from this gifted but often overlooked giant of silent comedy is on the way.

For sheer laugh content, few comedians hit the bull's eye more consistently than Laurel and Hardy. The most successful comic duo in cinema history, they navigated the precarious silent-to-sound transition more successfully than any of their contemporaries. While some voice a preference for the team's talking films, Stan and Ollie's silents undeniably contain a magic all their own.

The comedic approach of Laurel and Hardy took root in the fertile ground of the Hal Roach studio. It was common in the silent era for leading performers to maintain a stable of gag men, skilled at keeping the creativity flowing. The Roach lot did this one better by having on hand some of the most fertile comedy minds in the business—comedian/director Charlie Chase, director Clyde Bruckman and production supervisor F. Richard Jones among them. Along with Laurel, whose acumen in screen comedy was second to none, this informal team crafted a unique approach to film funny business that set the studio apart from other, more imitative comedy factories.

Laurel & Hardy in *You're Darn Tootin'*

One component of this style was the "tit for tat" conflict with an unexpected adversary. Unfolding at a deliberate and measured pace, the clash was usually sparked by some minor misunderstanding. But pride, of course, demands retribution, usually at an escalated level to elicit some measure of personal satisfaction. Soon enough the cycle spirals out of control and, in wonderful two-reelers like *Two Tars, You're Darn Tootin'* and the undisputed classic *Big Business*, the mayhem unleashed by Laurel and Hardy begins to take its toll on innocent bystanders and personal property. Although it may sound formulaic, the execution of this routine was performed with pleasing variation, making it always appear fresh and inspired.

Laurel and Hardy's performing skill was also an important element in their style. Unlike the typical screen duo, in which a comic clown was paired with a straight man, this team featured two performers who were equally capable of delivering a visual punch line. Stan

Laurel's screen repertoire was as pleasing as it was varied—his vacant expression, looks of perplexity and childlike whimper are among the beloved images of classic comedy. Equally impressive are the onscreen reactions of Oliver Hardy. His proud tie-twiddle, expressions of shame and silent pleas for audience sympathy became standard fixtures of the team's popular two-reelers. Providing a contrast to their screen relationship is the hostility of Edgar Kennedy, Charlie Hall, James Finlayson and other familiar faces from the Hal Roach roster. Watch films like *Liberty* or *Wrong Again* and experience firsthand the wonderful interplay of this talented group of performers.

Laurel and Hardy on top of the world in *Liberty*

Given the importance of Laurel and Hardy's silent comedies, the present unavailability of their work on DVD borders on the criminal. Long out of print is Image Entertainment's *Lost Films of Laurel and Hardy* series, which packaged many of their silents with other early Hal Roach two-reelers. Hallmark Incorporated, which currently owns the rights to the Roach film catalog, has expressed little interest in making these treasures available, save for last year's half-hearted DVD release that included the talkie feature *Sons of the Desert* with a handful of sound-era shorts. The Kino/Lobster collaboration (there's that name again) is compiling several of Laurel's early solo works for the upcoming DVD release, *The Stan Laurel Collection*. Currently, however, the best bet for Laurel and Hardy fans are the Region 2 DVD releases now available in Europe. Companies like Kinowelt (Germany), Universal/Benelux (the Netherlands) and Universal/Vision Video (the United Kingdom) have produced lavish DVD sets that package the team's short and feature length films in a variety of configurations. Those with an all-region DVD player can seek out these collections; all others must wait to see if similar releases will eventually be made available in North America.

At one time, Roscoe Arbuckle was among the most popular film comics in the world. Known to the public as "Fatty" (a moniker he detested), Arbuckle reached the heights of comedy stardom through his work at Keystone and later at Comique, the company established to produce his popular two-reelers. Although scandal and an unjust ban from moviemaking brought an abrupt halt to his performing career, Roscoe's early work is proof of his formidable screen talents.

To the uninitiated, Arbuckle's versatility comes as a revelation. With the agility of a ballroom dancer, he executed the most demanding of physical gags effortlessly, with expert timing and a pleasing comic flourish. Appearing in drag was a common convention during this period, but Roscoe topped this by appearing convincingly as a female character

Roscoe on a wild ride in *Fatty at Coney Island*

Arbuckle with long-time partner Mable Normand

comedy king Charlie Chaplin; their 1914 collaboration *The Rounders* is a wonder of mugging and mutual scene stealing. Last, but certainly not least, is a series of films made with rising comic Buster Keaton at the Comique film factory. In *The Bell Boy*, *Good Night Nurse!* and *The Garage*, one can observe Arbuckle at the top of his game with Keaton catching up quickly.

Time has passed and Roscoe Arbuckle now stands once again alongside the other comedy legends of early film. Many of his Sennett-era shorts have been released in DVD collections like Image Entertainment's five-disc *Slapstick Encyclopedia*. His Comique teamings with Buster Keaton are also available in standalone discs from both Image and Kino. As of this writing, only his later Paramount features are conspicuously absent from the DVD scene. While much of early film comedy has dated badly, Arbuckle's screen work remains as inventive and appealing as ever.

in titles like *Miss Fatty's Seaside Lovers*. His skill as a director also won acclaim. Many of his self-directed shorts contain sequences that display delightfully inventive imagery, such as the camera that tilts upward as he is about to disrobe in *The Knockabout* or the valentine-shaped cutout used to introduce onscreen sweetheart Mabel Normand in *Fatty and Mabel Adrift.*

Arbuckle's films also benefited from the presence of other familiar comedy faces. His lengthy partnership with the aforementioned Mabel Normand was one of the first screen pairings to enter the collective cultural consciousness. Supporting work from Sennett veteran Ford Sterling and real-life nephew Al St. John also provided much grist for the comedy mill. While at Keystone, Roscoe worked briefly with

Buster Keaton and Arbuckle

Max Linder and Ethel the lioness in *Seven Years' Bad Luck*

Max and His Mother-in-Law (*Max et sa belle mere*, France, 1910)

History demands the inclusion of Max Linder on any comprehensive list of silent comedy legends. In a series of films released through Pathe, Linder established himself as a worldwide comedy icon, a situation that belies his relative obscurity today. Even Chaplin himself acknowledged his debt to this important influence from the early years of the cinema.

An import from France, Max combined a sophisticated screen image with a preference for elaborate sight gags. Elements of farce also enter into his plots. In *Max Takes a Bath*, Linder must fill up his new bathtub in the hallway of his apartment building; the filled tub is too heavy to carry inside, forcing Max to bathe in a very public manner. *Max's Hat* is mishandled in a variety of ways until a passing dog finally gives it the "lifted leg" treatment (and you thought that bathroom humor was a recent invention!). A drunken Max Linder is attired in a suit of armor in *Max and the Statue* when he passes out and is delivered to an art gallery. Through improbable but imaginative scenarios like these, Linder set the standard for many screen comics to follow.

Max's dapper look made him a natural for stories involving marital misunderstandings and battles of the sexes. Linder's honeymoon plans take a serious setback when he is cajoled into bringing along his wife's mother in *Max and His Mother-in-Law*. One of his later features, *Be My Wife*, finds him going to similarly ridiculous extremes to romance his girlfriend. It would be years before Hollywood would master such genteel situation comedies; by that time, Max Linder already had it down to a science.

Much of Linder's work survives only in fragmentary form, making it impossible to compile a comprehensive overview of his work. Image Entertainment has attempted to remedy this with a DVD release entitled *Laugh With Max Linder*, which includes a restoration of *Seven Years' Bad Luck* along with four silent shorts. The same company's massive *Slapstick Encyclopedia* also contains an abridgment of the feature *Be My Wife*. Like a number of film comics, Max Linder wrote, directed and produced much of his own work. Such a versatile talent deserves not to be forgotten.

Charlie Chaplin and Max Linder

Appreciation for the talents of Harry Langdon has waxed and waned over the years. A comedian whose film career imploded when he parted ways with his creative team, Langdon went on to have an undistinguished career in

Harry Langdon takes a break with Ollie and Stan on the set of *Chumps at Oxford*. Langdon was a screenwriter on the film.

the sound era. But during the silent years, he was one of the bright lights of film comedy.

At the Sennett studio, Langdon developed a quirky but likable screen persona—that of a helpless man-child, forever at the mercy of the world, yet surviving with the aid of providence. This identity was first explored in shorts like *All Night Long*, which finds soldier boy Harry manning the "Suicide Post" at the front lines and, through dumb luck, surviving to win accolades for his exploits. In *Saturday Afternoon*, Langdon is cajoled by ne're-do-well Vernon Dent into (innocently) straying from his wife; his comeuppance inevitably comes, of course, in hilarious fashion. Although approaching middle age, Harry had a baby-faced appearance that made onscreen predicaments like these all the more compelling.

Langdon experienced his greatest commercial success with a series of features made at Sennett and First National. Bizarre situations and sight gags provide these films with some of their best moments. *His First Flame* contains a sequence showing a miniature Harry as an infant in a cradle, as bemused at the world as ever. In *Tramp, Tramp, Tramp*, he is involved in a prison break when serendipity provides an unexpected way of breaking free from his manacles. Langdon must fill in for the title circus act in the final reel of *The Strong Man*; the resulting sequence is visual comedy at its most inspired.

With Langdon riding this wave of cinematic momentum, few could have envisioned the manner in which his career would suddenly get off track. From the beginning, Harry benefited from the presence of a productive support team—director Harry Edwards and writers Arthur Ripley and soon-to-be legend Frank Capra (who later took over for Edwards). After the filming of the feature *Long Pants*, clashes with the comedy star triggered the departure of Capra, who later characterized Langdon as being the victim of an oversized ego. Harry's subsequent films faltered and he wound down his career making lowly two-reelers for Educational and Columbia, one of the most precipitous falls for any silent clown.

But Harry Langdon's prime work is still essential viewing for fans of classic comedy. The Image Entertainment release *Harry Langdon...The Forgotten Clown* contains his three best features, *Tramp, Tramp, Tramp, The Strong Man* and *Long Pants* on a single DVD. A mix of Harry's work from the Sennett period is also available on the *Slapstick Encyclopedia*, available from the same company. See the films and decide for yourself if Langdon was truly one of the greats.

Upon hearing the name Raymond Griffith, most film historians hang their heads in lament. So many of Griffith's films are lost that it is impossible to appraise his career in any meaningful fashion. But what we have is so intriguing, and the surviving reviews so favorable, that there is likely some justification for including him on a list of the most significant silent comedians.

Griffith put in stints at Sennett, Goldwyn and Universal before hitting his stride in a series of features at Paramount. Similar to William Powell in both manner and appearance, Griffith possessed a suave, carefree screen persona, adept at finding his way both in and out of trouble. Some details of his career are in dispute, owing to the unavailability of his work and to the fact that fellow associates regarded him as being somewhat loose with the truth. But it is known that Griffith acquired much experience while working with Max Sennett, writing, directing and gaining a mastery of comedy production to supplement his skills as a performer.

And of his work, what does survive? Some of his early films for Keystone are extant, such as *A Scoundrel's Toll* and *His Foot-Hill Folly*. *Changing Husbands*, a Leatrice Joy farce in which Griffith plays a supporting role, also makes the rounds in film collector's circles, as does the comedy/mystery *You'd Be Surprised*. A more accurate indication of Raymond Griffith's screen talents can be seen in his few Paramount features that are available. *Paths to Paradise* is a joyous romp, with Griffith cast as a carefree jewel thief who engages in burglary for the sheer hell of it—even with a missing reel, the film makes for satisfying viewing. *Hands Up!*,

Griffith's best-known work, has a Civil War setting that finds him searching for a hidden supply of gold to fund the Union war effort. Unfortunately, other well-regarded titles like *A Regular Fellow, Wet Paint* and *Wedding Bells* are presently nowhere to be found.

Given the scarcity of Raymond Griffith's surviving titles, an official DVD release is almost certainly out of the question. Enterprising film viewers can seek out his titles via the still thriving bootleg market on either VHS or DVD-R. It's a shame that some of Griffith's most popular films now appear to be lost forever. But it's an even greater shame that so few have seen the surviving work of this important and nearly forgotten screen comic.

One of the more successful of the second-string silent comedians was Hal Roach regular Charley Chase. A personal favorite of this writer, Chase was a multi-talented performer whose popularity never quite reached critical mass. His films, however, are consistently entertaining and occasionally inventive on a level that would make even the acknowledged comedy masters proud.

Charley Chase tries to spend more time with his son (Mickey Bennett) after a separation from his wife (Katherine Grant) even though his battle-ax mother-in-law (Josephine Crowell) tries to keep the family apart in *No Father to Guide Him*.

After cutting his comedic teeth at Keystone, Chase became a key contributor to the Roach fun factory. When not appearing in front of the camera, he divided his time between writing, directing and devising gags for the other players on the lot. (In his later sound films, Chase was also able to show off a dulcet singing voice.) Brash, but always personable, Charley's screen image was that of an everyman, scheming his way from one predicament to the next, but seldom achieving the outcome that he expected.

The comedy of embarrassment was Charley Chase's forte. Charley takes his onscreen son to the beach in *No Father to Guide Him* and loses his swimming trunks in the process. The hilarious but seldom screened *Limousine Love* finds Chase on his way to his wedding when, unbeknownst to him, a naked girl has slipped into the back seat of his auto (try explaining that to the in-laws!). An extra bonus in his films is the presence of lovelies from the Hal Roach lot like Anita Garvin, Vivien Oakland and Thelma Todd, who turn up with pleasing frequency.

Surrealism also sends the fun meter careening off the chart. Sequences like the final reel gag in *Mighty Like a Moose*, in which Charley stages a fight with himself to ward off the suspicions of a distrusting wife, must be seen to be believed.

To familiarize yourself with the work of this fine comedian, keep an eye out for *The Charley Chase Collection*. This upcoming release, which will package seven of his silent shorts on a single DVD, is another offering from that ambitious Kino/Lobster combo (try ordering that

Unfortunately, today Max Davidson's films are considered politically incorrect and difficult to find.

at your favorite seafood restaurant!). Chase's career extended well into sound films, where he appeared in short comedies for both Roach and Columbia until his death in 1940. Both his silent and sound films offer untold hours of laughter for inquisitive film fans.

At a time when the forces of political correctness threaten to whitewash all traces of ethnicity from the movie screen, the comedies of Max Davidson are as indispensable as lox on a bagel. Wearing his Jewish identity like a prayer shawl, Davidson's films remind us that the cinema once celebrated ethnic differences with gales of laughter that could bring an audience together.

With his full beard and expressive body language, Davidson took traditional stereotypes and turned them on their head. After witnessing a road accident in *Jewish Prudence*, Max connives his son into faking a leg injury; the resulting trial is a disaster of comic proportions. Wedding bells chime for Max and a rich widow in *Don't Tell Everything*, providing he can keep the new Mrs. Davidson away from his mischievous son. One of my favorite lines in all of silent comedy is the title card that introduces a cold, shivering Max in the feature *Sunshine of Paradise Alley*: "Levy—one of God's frozen people."

As with the best Roach comedies, plots and characterization in the Max Davidson films are always believable, with humor provided by wonderfully executed sight gags. In *Call of the Cuckoo*, Max moves into his new house, which is a nightmare of crisscrossed wiring, uneven floors and generally wacky construction. Perhaps the height of Maxian madness is the two-reeler *Pass the Gravy*, in which Davidson unknowingly serves up his neighbor's prized bantam rooster for dinner. This film is so well regarded by knowledgeable cinephiles it has been selected for inclusion into the Library of Congress' prestigious National Film Registry.

The films of Max Davidson, unfortunately, have also fallen into the black hole of DVD unavailability. This is not surprising, given his relative obscurity and the overtly ethnic nature of his humor in these sensitive times. In the late 1920s, Max Davidson embraced his heritage, inviting viewers to laugh at him and with him. Today, those who are motivated to seek out his work on bootleg VHS or DVD-R are invited to do the same, modern political sensibilities be damned.

Any comprehensive list of silent comedians needs to make note of additional performers not listed above. Lupino Lane, Lloyd Hamilton, Snub Pollard, Ben Turpin and Colleen Moore, among others, also left their collective mark of laughter on the cinema of the 1920s. Availability of their work is variable, but enough is extant to keep a film fan busy for many a happy viewing session.

Trends in humor come and go. Popular faces may soon be forgotten. But the comedies of the silent era remain the bedrock on which much of later Hollywood comedy was based. This is no mere hyperbole—eagle-eyed viewers will quickly spot gags and comedic situations that would be copied freely during the later sound era. Watch for yourself and see how much richer the joy was the first time around.

Go ahead. You could probably use a good laugh.

LIONEL ATWILL'S SERIAL ADVENTURES

by Todd M. Gault

Ah, the serials. No other genre ever contained more action and excitement in the space of 15 to 20 minutes than the lowly serial. Those weekly installments of comic book mayhem might have been looked down upon as the lowest form of filmmaking by the industry, but they were a proving ground for up and coming stars like John Wayne, or a safe haven for stars whose careers were on the way down like Lionel Atwill.

After a highly publicized sex scandal, Atwill found himself playing smaller and smaller parts in horror films. Where he had been a headliner in such films, Atwill was now barely garnering five minutes of screen time. Though he was not a star in features anymore, the same could not be said of the serials Atwill began making in the early 1940s.

Atwill's first serial was for the company he is most associated with, Universal Pictures. He was just coming off one of his last major roles in a horror film, *The Ghost of Frankenstein* (1942), when Universal cast him in *Junior G-Men of the Air* (1942) as The Baron, a super Japanese spy out to wreak havoc on American soil. Atwill was sixth billed after the members of The Little Tough Guys.

The Little Tough Guys were made up of four of the Warner Bros. Dead End Kids from the 1930s. After Warner Bros. dropped the group, Leo Gorcey and Bobby Jordan moved to Monogram and put together The East Side Kids, which later morphed into The Bowery Boys. The remaining members, Billy Halop, Huntz Hall, Gabriel Dell and Bernard Punsley went to Universal and the short-lived Little Tough Guys series. After the series ended Hall, and later Dell, would join Gorcey at Monogram. Besides making a string of features, The Little Tough Guys made three serials, *Junior G-Men of the Air* was the last, and a follow up to their first serial, *Junior G-Men* (1940).

The plot concerned the gang, who are working at an auto and plane junkyard, getting involved with Axis agents, when Halop's brother invents a new airplane engine and decides to give it to the government for the war effort. When things get dangerous, the gang is approached by a teen who represents the Junior G-Men of America, where after some initial hesitation about helping the cops, Halop and the rest join the organization and enthusiastically track down the spies.

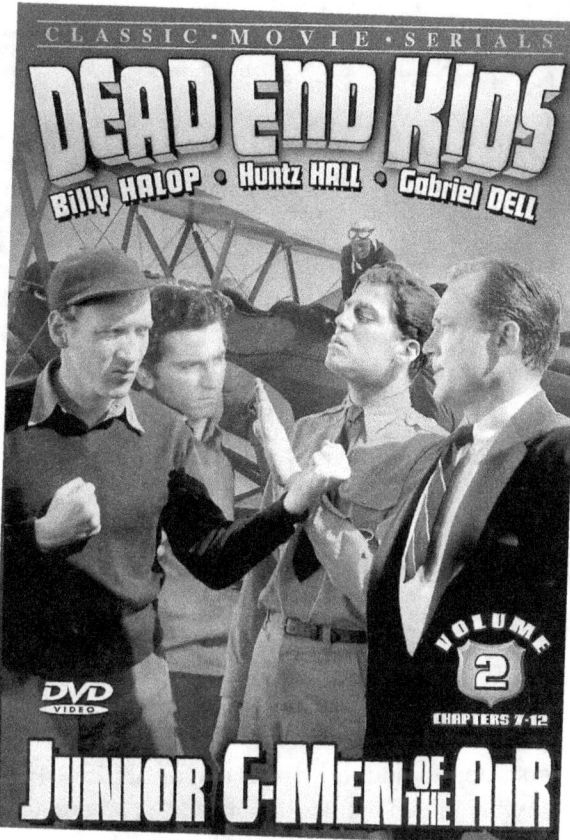

Since the serial was a vehicle for the still-popular youths, it was more of a showcase for their antics than Atwill's effortless villainy. The plot follows the same formula of all their serials. The Little Tough Guys are a group of poor kids from the wrong side of the tracks who have a deep distrust of all authority figures. After a few scuffles with the bad guys, and some voiced reluctance, they will then join forces with an adult, and after working together, both groups come to a better understanding about each other.

Universal was going through some changes in its serial department at this time. During the 1930s, the studio had been the leader in the field thanks to their adaptation of comic strips like *Tailspin Tommy* (1934) and *Flash Gordon* (1936). But as the decade moved to a close, and most of the small independent studios that made serials had disappeared, another major studio entered the serial arena, Columbia Pictures. Even worse for Universal, a new studio, Republic Pictures, had started up and was making better serials than either company, with less money.

So Universal decided to change the look of its serials to better compete with the competition by looking different, and perhaps easing its budget constraints. Republic was making the best all around action films in the business and Columbia's serials were turned into over-the-top farces by director James W. Horne. So Universal, always a company that had put more emphasis on plot than other studios, began to pull back on the action and concentrate more on the characters. As a consequence, their serials began to be overburdened with dialogue.

A typical chapter would have a little action in the beginning as the previous episode's cliffhanger was resolved, then all of the characters would discuss what was going on and the villains would come up with a plan, after which the episode ended with another cliffhanger. What action there was in the film was composed of footage either taken from an earlier serial, or from a larger-budgeted feature film.

While this may have slowed down the action, it did allow for more adult themes to slip

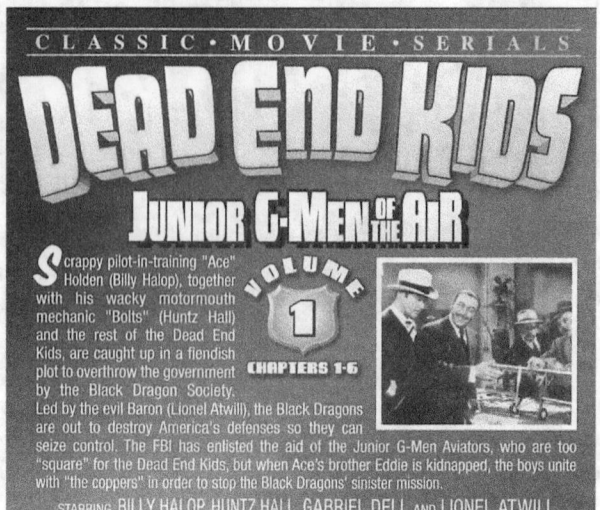

CLASSIC · MOVIE · SERIALS

DEAD END KIDS

JUNIOR G-MEN OF THE AIR

VOLUME 1 — CHAPTERS 1-6

Scrappy pilot-in-training "Ace" Holden (Billy Halop), together with his wacky motormouth mechanic "Bolts" (Huntz Hall) and the rest of the Dead End Kids, are caught up in a fiendish plot to overthrow the government by the Black Dragon Society. Led by the evil Baron (Lionel Atwill), the Black Dragons are out to destroy America's defenses so they can seize control. The FBI has enlisted the aid of the Junior G-Men Aviators, who are too "square" for the Dead End Kids, but when Ace's brother Eddie is kidnapped, the boys unite with "the coppers" in order to stop the Black Dragons' sinister mission.

STARRING BILLY HALOP, HUNTZ HALL, GABRIEL DELL and LIONEL ATWILL

into the mix. Billy Halop best exemplifies this. Always an underrated actor, Halop easily shows the character's inner turmoil between remaining true to the street code he has grown up with and choosing to do his part for his country in its time of need, or in other words, taking that first step to adulthood and responsibility. If anything mars the performance, it is a certain lack of freshness, as Halop had played the same type of character in two previous serials and was obviously becoming tired of it.

But as this is an action film aimed at youngsters, such mature themes are kept on the fringe. Helping to keep the kids in the audience from being too bored by all the talk is Huntz Hall, who was in the middle of his transformation from street punk to goofy comedy relief. He hadn't evolved into the slightly effeminate and brain-dead Sach of The Bowery Boys at this point (Hall's work in The Bowery Boys is like the comedy of The Three Stooges—you either love him or can't stand him, there's is no middle ground). Here Hall is still the tough-talking teen hood, but occasionally he gets in a funny wisecrack at someone's expense. The funniest thing about Hall's character is wondering how he is able to keep his ball cap on while flying in a plane with an open cockpit. That is when you're not wondering how a kid who works in a junkyard learned to fly in the first place.

Atwill doesn't fare half as well as the post-teen actors do. The great thespian is saddled with a blatantly obvious wig of black hair and the Japanese makeup pulls his skin so tight toward the back of his head that his eyes are practically closed. Atwill doesn't help matters himself. He so overacts as to make his character ludicrous. He is all huge grins and cunning chuckles. The only saving grace in his performance is that he doesn't attempt to hide his English accent with a Japanese one, or talk in pidgin English. Instead, he prefers to speak in a stilted manner, as if he is unfamiliar with the language. This is by far the worst performance Atwill ever gave in any film.

First-time viewers will be a little taken aback to notice male Universal sex symbol Turhan Bey popping up as a minor Japanese spy. His early days at the studio were filled with such appearances in their wartime-themed films and serials.

Though not as action-packed as Universal's earlier work, the serial is well directed by Ray Taylor and Lewis D. Collins. It was a standard practice to usually have two directors work on a serial; one would film action scenes with the stuntmen while the other would handle scenes of dialogue. This allowed for an economical use of time as most serials only had a three- to four-week shooting schedule, with retakes being practically unheard of.

Ray Taylor was one of the most prolific directors of serials from the silent days through the mid-1940s and worked for most of the studios that made serials. He was an experienced director of action films and any thrills that come from the production are a testament to Taylor's skill and talent when given dialogue-heavy material.

This was Lewis D. Collins' first collaboration with Ray Taylor. Though inexperienced at this time, he would quickly become adept at making action films and help Taylor helm 12 serials over a four-year period. It would be Taylor's longest partnership in the genre.

Atwill's second foray into the field was Republic Pictures' adaptation of Marvel (then know as Timely) Comics' wartime creation *Cap-*

tain America (1944). Though Atwill was third billed under Dick Purcell and Lorna Gray, company records show he was the highest-paid actor on the production.

Atwill portrayed museum curator Dr. Maldor who, feeling that his colleagues from a jungle expedition had cheated him out of money and glory, wages a campaign of terror and murder under the guise of The Scarab. Battling him is crusading District Attorney Grant Gardner, who also has a secret identity, that of Captain America.

Anyone familiar with the comic book can tell right away that Republic made a few cosmetic changes to the superhero. Gone is the Army setting, the name of Steve Rogers and sidekick Bucky Barnes. The look of the character's costume is also drastically changed. Gone are the wings on the mask, the buccaneer-style boots, and, most glaringly, his shield, which was replaced by something more in keeping with other Republic heroes, a revolver.

Apparently Marvel had never looked to see what changes Republic made with other characters they adapted, like *The Lone Ranger* and *Captain Marvel*, and didn't even check on the production until filming was almost completed. When Marvel finally did protest what had been done, Republic responded by stating that the changes Marvel had requested would be too expensive to make; and since their contract didn't explicitly state how the character was to be handled, Republic wasn't going to do anything about it. Ironically, Marvel hadn't even asked for any money from the film company for use of the character. Republic's payment for *Captain America* was to simply advertise the serial in the comic book.

Putting aside any preconceived notions about what the character is supposed to be, the serial is a great piece of action filmmaking thanks to directors John English and Elmer Clifton. Both directors are veterans of serial production. Elmer Clifton worked mainly in the 1930s on films made by small, independent companies, this being his first serial in five years. It would also be his last. English was a true veteran at Republic who had just come off a major run with the man many consider the best director of serials, William Witney. From 1937 until 1941, when the studio broke up the partnership, the two men collaborated on 17 productions, all of them classics.

Both English and Clifton keep the plot constantly moving in this slickly made production. Each episode contains a furious fistfight between Captain America and never fewer than two opponents. The stunt work on these fights is eye-popping. They range over entire rooms, with fists seeming to knock opponents over tables and furniture, leaving most sets in shambles. Republic had pioneered the concept of having a stunt man double actors for dangerous stunts. They hired stunt ace Yakima Canutt

Lionel Atwill as the ruthless villain in *Captain America*

to create a team of stunt performers when the studio was founded in 1936. Witney and English worked out how to choreograph and film fight scenes based on the concepts Busby Berkley used to make his musicals.

The best fight is in the last chapter. It contains the most set destruction and most interesting choreography. But what really makes it stand out are the participants. The fight is between 59-year-old Lionel Atwill (doubled by Fred Graham) and Captain America (doubled by Dale Van Sickle). After having spent the previous 14 chapters watching the costumed hero make mincemeat out of two or three opponents at a time, it is almost surreal to watch the stuntman who is supposed to be Atwill all but mop the floor with the younger man. The hero takes enough chair shots to cause Mick Foley to cringe.

When characters aren't fighting, they are shooting at each other. First-time viewers will be a little shocked to see Captain America whip out a gun and start blasting away. But he isn't the only one—everybody in this film seems to carry a gun and doesn't hesitate to use it. *Captain America* contains probably the largest body count other than a war picture—the death toll averages at least two people per chapter. Two to three people being gunned down in every chapter seems a bit excessive since serials were targeted mainly for children.

The performances are pretty good. Dick Purcell is an effective and ingratiating lead; Lorna Gray, though not given much to do other than be put in danger, does what she can to make her one-dimensional character seem interesting; and George J. Lewis as Atwill's main henchman, who is an oily and sadistic thug, is rock solid.

But Atwill, with very little effort, blows them all off the screen. Though ill during the filming, the thespian gives a strong and multilayered performance. It is his best work in a serial, and the best work he had done since his early 1940s Universal films. While most serial villains give an overly flamboyant portrayal, Atwill takes the opposite route. Always calm and self assured, he rarely even raises his voice, preferring to let his tone convey the true menace.

One of the most shocking scenes occurs in Chapter 13, where Atwill decides to torture information out of John Hamilton (TV's Perry White of *Superman* fame), by using a bullwhip. The camera stays on Atwill as he takes off his jacket and slowly rolls up his sleeve, leaving on his riding glove. Then with quiet deliberation, he proceeds to repeatedly slash the whip at the suspended victim, all the while never changing his expression of mild curiosity. The scene was clearly filmed to remind audiences of Atwill's horror resume, as are scenes where he uses a stolen invention to revive a dead Lewis and the climax that has Gray locked in a glass case, which fills with a gas that will shrivel her into a mummy. Ironically, Universal never seemed to want to capitalize on Atwill's horror status, even though they were the house of Dracula and Frankenstein. Horror fans, if they keep a sharp eye out, will catch sight of Robert Frazer from *White Zombie* (1932) as the inventor of the resurrecting machine. Audiences might not recognize him, as he hadn't aged very well since the early 1930s. In fact he ended up playing haggard old men in serials as early as 1936.

If there are any complaints about this serial it is the character of Captain America. No reason is ever given why crime fighter Grant Gardner felt the necessity to dress up in red, white, and blue tights. We would like to know his reason for putting on a disguise, although none is offered. Everything the hero does in costume, he also does out of costume, making the whole point superfluous.

Atwill returned to Universal for his last two serials, which would re-team him with director Ray Taylor and Lewis D. Collins. First up was *Raiders of Ghost City* (1944), Atwill's only Western.

While Westerns have been a major portion of most studios' serial output, their plots are more repetitive than other serials, due to the limited variations inherent in a Western story. Sometimes this is overcome by infusing the serial with science fiction elements, or, as in this film, by including topical references. What really sets *Raiders of Ghost City* apart is that it is set in the last days of the Civil War.

Universal's Western serials were always complexly plotted, and this one is no exception. Atwill plays Alex Morel, who runs a saloon in the small town of Oro Grande. Morel is in the pay of the Confederate Army and gathers information about Union gold shipments. Confederate Captain Clay Randolph (Regis Toomey) uses the information to lead a daring series of raids to help fund the Confederate Army. Union Captain Steve Clark (Dennis Moore), a West Point classmate of Randolph's, is dispatched to stop the raids. During the course of the serial the War ends and Randolph, who has decided

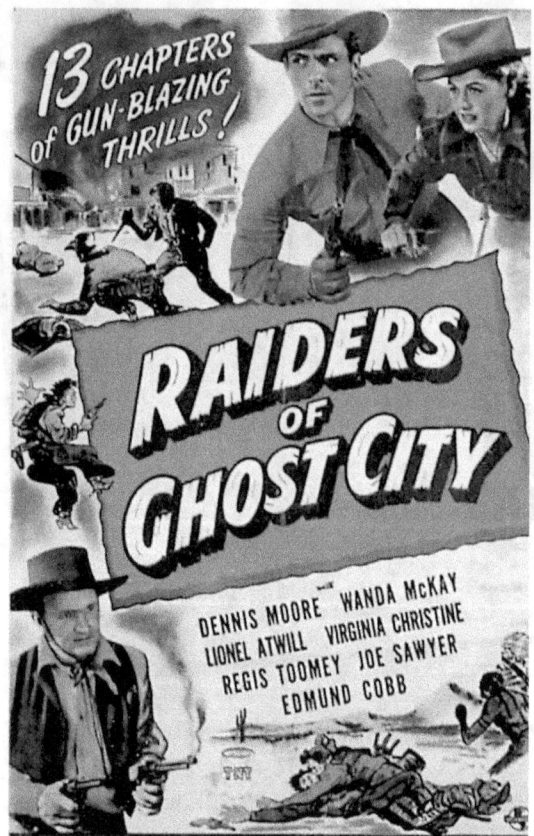

Unfortunately, the acting is another matter. As the hero, Dennis Moore has plenty of screen time, but isn't able to hold the audience's attention. Popular in B-westerns and horror films, Moore was blessed with a deep, pleasing voice. The only thing he lacked was personality. Moore can say any line with absolute conviction—but with almost no emotion. He was the blandest of the bland.

Regis Toomey, on the other hand, gives the best performance in the serial. He effectively expresses his character's inner conflict between his cause and his old friend. In the end he resolves to obey orders. He shows sadness as well as relief when the war ends, his cause is lost, but he regains his friendship with Steve Clark.

Atwill doesn't fare as well. He is ill used by the filmmakers, who don't allow him to show his genius at villainy. He is little more than ingratiating when confronted by the heroes, and scowl slightly when he is in his hidden headquarters. What's missing from the performance is that sly Atwill wit. The exception is the Chapter One cliffhanger where the hero is

to turn himself in to Clark, is killed by Morel, who wants the gold raids to continue. What no one knows is that Morel is a German spy sent to America to steal gold so that Germany can buy Alaska from Russia!

The Civil War setting cannot disguise the implication that this serial is really about World War II. The real villains are undercover agents from Germany, or American thugs duped into thinking they are stealing gold for themselves. While the serial is most concerned about making disparaging comments about Germans, the filmmakers also use the setting to show how loyal Americans band together in times of trouble. Such motivations were rare in serials, where issues tended toward a simplistic black and white viewpoint.

Directors Taylor and Lewis keep things moving despite having a script that is filled with dialogue and plot twists. The action is well handled, and the close-ups of Dennis Moore and Joe Sawyer, as Moore's sidekick Idaho Jones, mesh well with footage from earlier serials.

Hero Dennis Moore manhandles bad guy Lionel Atwill in *Raiders of Ghost City.*

trapped in a runaway railroad car, which zooms down a steep hill while our hero battles several villains. When the car first comes away from the rest of the train, Atwill is seen entering a car while casually wiping his hands. He turns to a waiting compatriot, played by fellow Universal horror alumnus Virginia Christie, and calmly remarks, "I'm afraid, my dear, that the coupling on the last car has come loose." It is a great scene, and the serial could have used more of them.

Another detriment to the serial is the plot. The Civil War and German agents parts are fine. The problem is the overall goal of the villains, stealing gold to buy Alaska. Since every schoolboy knows that the U.S.A. actually bought Alaska in 1867, it kills any suspense the audience might have had over whether or not the good guys win. Okay, I know that all serials end with the good guys winning and the bad guys losing, and that fans watch them knowing this in advance. But the problem here is that the plot stretches the viewer's suspension of disbelief, and the result is a lack of interest in the overall story.

Atwill's final serial, *Lost City of the Jungle* (1946), is just sad. He died of pneumonia/cancer before the serial was completed. This was a blow to the filmmakers—serials didn't have the budget to handle such a massive amount of re-shooting with another actor, nor could they afford to just scrap the production. They came up with two solutions to complete the production. One was to hire an actor who resembled Atwill from the back. In some scenes, a henchman faces the camera, asks a question or reports an event to the stand-in, which would then be intercut with close-ups of Atwill. It was usually the same shot each time, as Atwill always had the same thoughtful expression before giving a slight nod. The other solution involved a rewrite, which introduced another character as Atwill's boss.

They got another lucky break in the way that serials were filmed. Originally all productions were filmed in sequential order. Directors started on page one and stopped on the last page. During the latter days of the 1920s,

Lionel Atwill was very ill during filming of *Lost City of the Jungle* and passed away during the production.

stuntman/actor/director Joe Bonomo came up with the idea of breaking the script up so that all the scenes that took place on one set would be filmed at the same time and would be edited into place later. This was a revolutionary idea that helped keep budgets down. What this meant for the beleaguered production of *Lost City of the Jungle* was that most of Atwill's scenes had already been completed, so that he could appear throughout the entire serial.

The plot is an amazing hodgepodge of different movie genres. It contains secret agents, angry jungle natives, an archeological expedition and a passing resemblance to *Casablanca* (1942). Atwill plays Sir Eric Hazarias, a notorious warmonger. After faking his own death, he

arrives in the city of Pendrang, which is located in a valley nestled in the middle of the Himalayan mountains. Pendrang is a Moroccan-style city, surrounded by a vast jungle, and ruled by a mysterious woman named Indra (Helen Bennett), who operates out of a casino.

Hazarias, now passing himself off as philanthropist Geoffrey London, has started an archeological excavation that is really just a cover for his search to find a radioactive metal called Meteorium 245, which is the only known defense against the atomic bomb. Just before winter cuts Pendrang off from the outside world until spring, United Peace Foundation agent Rod Stanton (Russell Hayden) arrives, hot on Hazarias' trail, and he joins up with undercover agent and Pendrang native, Tal Shan (Keye Luke). What no one has yet discovered, except for the wily Indra, is that Hazarias is just a front for the real leader of the organization, his personal secretary Halborn (John Mylong, best known for appearing in 1953's *Robot Monster*).

Taylor and Lewis, in their last collaboration, do their best with the material, but there are too many diverse elements to make a really good serial. What the serial really lacks is the guiding hand of executive producer Henry McRae. McRae had been the force behind Universal serials since 1917, and he had been instrumental in getting the genre back on its feet when the coming of sound looked to be the end of serials. Unfortunately McRae died in 1944 after completing *Mystery of the Riverboat*.

Not that McRae could have done much if he had been alive. Universal was in the midst of merging with International Pictures to create Universal-International Pictures, and the first thing the new studio heads did was to close down the serial production unit at the end of the year.

Most of the acting is poor. Both Hayden and Mylong come across as lifeless; their brief confrontation scenes together lack any spark or tension. Hayden (coming off a run as William Boyd's sidekick in the Hopalong Cassidy films) isn't too bad, he just doesn't have enough acting ability to carry a lead. Keye Luke is much more memorable than Hayden, but then Luke was always an actor who could stand out in a scene. Mylong gives the worst performance in the film. It wouldn't have been so bad if he had been like Hayden, and just said his lines, but no, Mylong has to infuse his character with all sorts of broad, overdone hand gestures. His stilted line delivery doesn't match the physical performance.

Atwill's villain dons a disguise in *Lost City of the Jungle.*

Then you have poor Jane Adams. A good actress, as seen from her sympathetic portrayal of a hunchbacked nurse in *House of Dracula* (1945), she is given little to do. Playing the concerned daughter of a missing archeologist kidnapped by Atwill, she spends the entire serial constantly bemoaning the fate of her missing father, coming off whiny and irritating.

As in *Captain America*, Atwill dominates every scene he has. As this is his last film, it is nice to see Atwill back in form. He is also given good dialogue, which suits his particular brand of screen villainy. He is at his best during a cat and mouse exchange with Hayden, who is trying to get Atwill to make a slip that will reveal his secret identity. Atwill is clearly the winner in these exchanges; deftly showing he knows what the other is doing, a sly smile plays across his face before he resumes his supposed persona. He shines in this scene as he pulls Hayden close with the start of conspiratorial whisper that eventually reveals nothing, then smugly walks away.

Lionel Atwill's sudden demise closed the door on any future bouts of screen villainy. Though many companies stopped making horror films after 1946, it is conceivable he might have continued appearing in serials for Republic and Columbia until the end of the decade. It is even possible he could have adapted his screen image to the sci-fi horror films of the 1950s and continued appearing in small roles for such studios as AIP or Astor.

But that is something we will never know. As it stands, he left behind a wonderful legacy of films full of rich performances. And that legacy includes his serials. They may not have been good roles, and seldom used him to his full potential, but they did give him decent-sized parts at a time when he needed the work. They are certainly worth a look by anyone who is interested in viewing some of the lesser-known films of this most distinctive of horror stars.

Resources:

Fifty Years of Serial Thrills, Roy Kinnard, The Scarecrow Press, Inc., 1983

The Great Movie Serials, Jim Harmon and Donald F. Glut, Doubleday and Company, Inc., 1972

In a Door, Into a Fight, Out a Door, Into a Chase, William Witney, McFarland and Company, Inc., 1996

In the Nick of Time, William C. Cline, McFarland and Company, Inc., 1984

Serial Adventures, James Van Hise, Pioneer Books, Inc., 1990

The Serials, Second Edition, Raymond W. Stedman, University of Oklahoma Press, 1977

Universal Horrors!, Michael Brunas, John Brunas and Tom Weaver, McFarland and Company, Inc., 1990

ALFRED HITCHCOCK'S SABOTEUR
BY MARK CLARK

Casual followers of Alfred Hitchcock's career may ask: "*Saboteur*? Is that the one where the little kid gets blown up, or the one where the guy falls off the Statue of Liberty?" (It's the one where the guy falls off the Statue of Liberty, but more on that later.)

Between his thrilling *The 39 Steps* in 1935 and the superb *North by Northwest* in 1959, Hitchcock brought *Saboteur*—another breathless, cross-country chase picture—to the screen in 1942. Unfortunately, the middle child of Hitchcock's pursuit trilogy never achieved the notoriety of its elder or younger siblings. Nowadays, *Saboteur* is often confused with Hitchcock's unrelated 1936 British movie, *Sabotage* (the one where the little kid gets blown up).

Unquestionably, both *The 39 Steps* (which is likely Hitchcock's finest British film) and *North by Northwest* (arguably the director's best film, period) are better pictures than *Saboteur*. But they're better pictures than nearly everything else, too. Removed from the shadows of its fabled brethren, *Saboteur* stands on its own as an important step in Hitchcock's artistic development, and as splendid entertainment.

The film might not exist at all, however, if Hitchcock's relationship with producer David O. Selznick had been more amicable. The two legendary moviemakers clashed like an argyle tie on a plaid shirt. Hitchcock desired more creative control than Selznick was comfortable surrendering.

Selznick, who brought Hitchcock to America in 1939, had little idea what to do with his gifted but temperamental director. The two men battled fiercely throughout the production of Hitchcock's first American film, *Rebecca* (1940), but wound up with an Oscar winner to their credit. After that arduous experience, however, Selznick grew content to loan Hitchcock out to other studios for a fee (per the terms of his contract with the director). *Saboteur*, filmed for Universal, was Hitchcock's fourth consecutive loan-out following the *Rebecca* ordeal.

By the time Hitchcock's contract with Selznick expired, he had collaborated with his celebrated producer on just three projects—*Rebecca*, *Spellbound* (1945) and *The Paradine Case* (1947)—but had been loaned out for seven other films. Ironically, most of the loan-outs were superior to the pictures Hitchcock and Selznick created together. Selznick never understood how to identify suitable material for Hitchcock's unique talent.

Certainly *Saboteur* was more Hitch's cup of tea than moribund fare like *The Paradine Case*. In fact, *Saboteur* could serve as a Hitchcock prototype.

Many themes which resurfaced throughout the director's career are present here: a man falsely accused of a heinous crime, who is then forced to capture the real criminal to prove his innocence; villains who appear to be upstanding citizens; a forced relationship which blossoms into a willing romance; characters trapped in a crowded, apparently friendly place; and, of course, the desperate overland pursuit. A few motifs from Hitchcock's earlier films (such as the handcuffs, a device lifted from *The 39 Steps*) reappear here; others (such as an action sequence set at a national landmark—the Statue of Liberty in this case; Mount Rushmore in *North by Northwest*) debut here, casting a template for later films.

Saboteur freed Hitchcock from Selznick's meddling but created new headaches all its own. Casting posed the biggest hurdle. Hitchcock wanted Gary Cooper and Barbara Stanwyck for the film's leads, but due to budget limitations had to settle for Robert Cummings and Priscilla Lane. He also envisioned casting Western hero Harry Carey against type as the film's chief villain, but Carey balked at the proposition. Suave Otto Kruger played Hitchcock's villain instead of folksy Carey.

As with many Hitchcock films (including both his other chase pictures), the story was built around a handful of preconceived set pieces, including its tense finale atop the Statue of Liberty. Stitching together a coherent narrative from these diverse parts proved daunting, and the script went through numerous rewrites. The final screenplay is

Hitchcock, his daughter Pat and Robert Cummings on the set of *Saboteur*, 1942

credited to Peter Viertel, Joan Harrison and Dorothy Parker. Parker—yes, that Dorothy Parker—came on board to punch up the film's dialogue. Hitchcock, who penned the original treatment and oversaw all the revisions, received no screen credit.

The story follows Barry Kane (Cummings), a blue-collar Everyman working in a California airplane factory during the early months of World War II. When the plant's paint shop catches fire, Barry and a friend, Ken Mason, rush to fight the blaze. A co-worker named Fry (Norman Lloyd) hands Barry a fire extinguisher, which Barry hands to Ken. Ken is killed in a sudden burst of flame. Fry disappears. Later, investigators learn the extinguisher had been filled with gasoline. When they can't find any record of an employee named Fry, they accuse Barry of sabotage and murder.

Kane hopes Mr. Tobin (Otto Kruger) will help prove his innocence.

Barry quickly surmises he must locate Fry to convince the police of the truth and the chase is on. Since Barry spotted a letter addressed to Fry from Deep Springs Ranch shortly before the fire at the plant, he decides to begin his search there. Barry thumbs a ride to the ranch with a truck driver (Murray Alper) who extols the virtues of keeping a fire extinguisher handy (!). Along the way, Barry endures a tense false alarm when the truck is pulled over by a motorcycle cop (foreshadowing *Psycho*).

Hitchcock populates *Saboteur* with fascinating villains, beginning with Mr. Tobin (Kruger, in the role originally designed for Carey). When we meet Tobin, proprietor of Deep Springs Ranch, he is playing with his granddaughter, a toddler named Suzy, in his swimming pool. Tobin claims to have never heard of Fry. Then Suzy accidentally reveals the truth, showing Barry a telegram from Fry to Tobin (with the message: "All finished here—Joining Nelson in Soda City").

Tobin instantly grows icy and smug. He calls the police, confident that authorities will not believe the ravings of a suspected saboteur over the word of a wealthy local citizen. Waiting for the cops to arrive, he discusses treason and murder with the same nonchalant smile he wore while playing with Suzy. Like Tobin, most of *Saboteur*'s villains are family men and apparently solid citizens.

"A man like you can't survive in a country like this," Barry warns Tobin, inaugurating one of the film's chief stumbling blocks: an overabundance of woefully dated wartime sloganeering. Shameless flag-waving served an important function at the time, fueling the fighting spirit of Americans after Japan's devastating attack on Pearl Harbor and other Pacific theater setbacks that befell American forces in 1941 and '42. But today the movie's ham-fisted patriotism seems naive at best.

Detectives handcuff Barry and shove him into a squad car, but our hero (still cuffed) bursts out of the vehicle and flees by leaping from a high bridge into a river below. Like Frankenstein's Monster, Barry finds refuge with a blind recluse. But his sanctuary is spoiled when the blind man's niece Pat (Lane) arrives. The old man, who for no good reason believes Barry is innocent, orders his niece to take Barry to a local blacksmith to have those pesky handcuffs removed. Pat figures (justifiably) that her uncle is off his nut, and decides to turn the suspected saboteur over to the police instead. Barry is forced to take Pat hostage and, in typical Hitchcock fashion, the two promptly begin falling in love.

Barry Kane (Robert Cummings) hitches a ride with Murray Alper.

Barry trashes Pat's car by using its fan to slice the chain connecting his handcuffs. So the couple bum a ride to Soda City with a busload of circus freaks. This far-fetched sequence features yet another close encounter with the cops, still more up-with-democracy sermonizing, as well as some memorable flourishes from Parker. Trapped in the desert, Pat whines about being cold:

> Barry: If you'd stop trying to be a hero and try being on my side, maybe we could do something about your being cold.
> Pat: Build a fire?
> Barry (eyeing Pat like a rabbit in a salad bar): No, I wasn't exactly thinking of that.

Parker also contributed some great lines for the circus performers, such as the Siamese twins who aren't on speaking terms with each other. One of the twins complains: "I wish you'd tell her to do something about her insomnia. I've done nothing but toss and turn all night."

This scene also reinforces another of Hitchcock's favorite themes; namely, that the finest people aren't the ones with the finest possessions. The respectable citizenry of *Saboteur* are either villains or hapless bystanders. The story's heroes, Barry and those who aid him in his just cause, are outcasts—a lonely trucker, a blind man, even circus freaks.

In Soda City, which turns out to be a ghost town, Barry and Pat discover a secret hideout stocked with everything a busy fifth columnist needs and even a couple of spies in residence. Pat escapes. Barry convinces the spies he's on their side (this being the one instance when it comes in handy to have your picture in the paper beneath a headline labeling you a traitor to your country). One of the men, Freeman (Alan Baxter), agrees to take Barry with him to "The Company's" New York headquarters. There's another nice touch here: During the trip to the Big Apple, Freeman explains that he has two sons, one of whom he keeps in long hair because he always wanted a daughter!

As soon as Freeman and guest arrive in New York, Tobin reappears and blows Barry's cover. Foolishly, Pat joins Barry at spy headquarters, a swank brownstone owned by wealthy philanthropist Mrs. Sutton (Alma Kruger). Tobin wants to execute

Pat (Priscilla Lane) helps Kane at the request of her blind uncle.

both Barry and Pat immediately, but squeamish Mrs. Sutton fears such gauche behavior would spoil the ritzy charity social she's busy hosting. While the villains debate, Barry whisks Pat out onto the crowded dance floor, where he tries to enlist partygoers' support. No one believes his crazy allegations about their esteemed hostess.

Mrs. Sutton (Alma Kruger) won't allow Tobin to execute Barry and Pat; it might spoil the society event she is hosting.

With the doors blocked by Mrs. Sutton's servants, Barry and Pat enjoy a passionate dance while trying to devise a means of escape. Suddenly one of Tobin's henchmen cuts in on Barry and whirls Pat away from the dance floor. Barry is apprehended as well, and imprisoned in a basement closet. He frees himself by setting off the fire alarm and escaping in the ensuing confusion. Barry attempts to prevent "The Company" from wrecking a new warship launching from the Brooklyn Navy Yard, but fails. In the attempt, however, he at last comes face to face with Fry, only to have the villain escape yet again.

Meanwhile, Pat also escapes. She's been working with the police since her arrival in New York, and with her help the cops round up Tobin's gang—except Fry. Barry, Pat and the police track Fry to the Statue of Liberty, setting up the film's famous climax.

This sequence provided the wellspring from which all other ideas in *Saboteur* flowed. Hitchcock wanted to film a man falling to his death, keeping the subject in focus all the way down so that audiences could see the stark terror on his face. Of course Hitch couldn't really toss a guy off the Statue of Liberty—the union would have a fit and there were no lenses capable of capturing the shot anyway.

Instead he made use of primitive blue-screen technology, filming Lloyd flailing and screaming, and imitating free fall in a rolling chair in front of a blue background. He filmed this sequence using a moving camera, which climbed a tall beam as Lloyd kicked and howled. Combining this footage with shots taken from atop the actual Statue of Liberty created a convincing process shot. Hitchcock would utilize similar trickery to create the famous *Vertigo* (1958) effect.

The sequence is much more than a technical exhibition, however. It's Hitchcock suspense at its most unsettling. The famed director lovingly structures every shot for maximum impact. Using another of his favorite devices, he removes almost all sound from this sequence. There's no music and almost no dialogue. We hear the distant moan of a tugboat and the song of passing seagulls. Such silence underscores the isolation, the helplessness one might feel in such a precarious position.

Barry confronts Fry on the torch of the Statue. Fry attempts to flee, stumbles and falls over the edge, but finds a tentative handhold on the sleeve of Lady Liberty. Barry—being the good sport that he is—climbs down and attempts to aid his nemesis, grabbing the sleeve of Fry's jacket to prevent the spy from falling. But slowly, agonizingly slowly, Fry's sleeve begins to separate from his jacket at the seams. After gasping—"Hurry… sleeve!"—Fry falls away, howling in terror.

Today *Saboteur* is likely remembered for this harrowing climax. Ironically, Hitchcock later felt he had botched this sequence. "From an audience point of view, I should have reversed the positions of Cummings and Norman Lloyd on the Statue of Liberty at the end of the picture," he told interviewer Peter Bogdanovich (as quoted in Bogdanovich's book, *Who the Devil Made It*). "The audience would have been much more anxious if the hero had been in danger, not the villain." Maybe so, but Hitchcock couldn't have let Cummings actually fall—negating the purpose of including the scene at all.

Saboteur was not a project Hitchcock held in high regard. The director was often a poor critic of his own work (mostly because he compared his films with his own mental vision of what he desired to create, rather than judging his finished movies on their own merits) but at least some of his complaints about *Saboteur* are valid.

For instance, the director remained bitter about having to settle for Cummings and Lane as the film's leads. "*Saboteur* was not successful in my mind because I don't think Robert Cummings was right," Hitchcock told Bogdanovich. "He was too undramatic, he had what I call a 'comedy face'." He elaborated with interviewer Francois Truffaut in Truffaut's book *Hitchcock/Truffaut*: "He (Cummings) is a competent performer, but he belongs in the light-comedy class of actors. Even when he's in desperate straits, his features don't convey anguish."

From this experience, Hitchcock told Truffaut, "I've learned...that whenever the hero isn't portrayed by a star the whole picture suffers, you see, because audiences are far less concerned about the predicament of a character who's played by someone they don't know."

Less convincingly, Hitchcock carps to Bogdanovich that Kruger was "all wrong" as Tobin. "What annoyed me the most was the casting of the heavy, Otto Kruger," he said. While Kruger didn't match Hitch's original conception of the character, he is simply terrific in the role, providing the film's most memorable performance. In fact, *Saboteur*'s greatest weakness is that its stereotype-twisting villains are far more interesting than its bland, bloodless heroes. That's a backhanded compliment to Kruger, as well as Lloyd and Baxter, all of whom act circles around the adequate but uninteresting Cummings and Lane.

Hitchcock's other major beef was with *Saboteur*'s script, which he felt was "cluttered" and

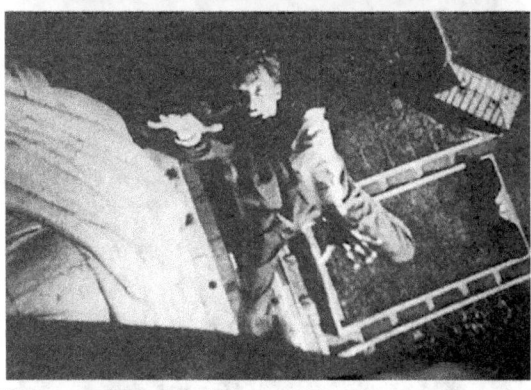

Barry confronts Fry (Norman Lloyd) on the Statue of Liberty in New York.

"undisciplined...The picture was overloaded with too many ideas," he told Bogdanovich. "Looking back on *Saboteur*, I would say the script lacks discipline," he told Truffaut:

Saboteur will be remembered for the harrowing climax at the Statue of Liberty.

"I don't think I exercised a clear, sharp approach to the original construction of the screenplay. There was a mass of ideas, but they weren't sorted out in proper order; they weren't selected with sufficient care. I feel the whole thing should have been pruned and tightly edited long before the actual shooting. It goes to show that a mass of ideas, however good

they are, is not sufficient to create a successful picture. They've got to be carefully presented with a consistent awareness of the shape of the whole."

Perhaps. But the over-crowded, picturesque narrative of *Saboteur* brings with it a quirky, manic *joi de vive* which would have been undercut by the carefully reasoned, streamlined approach Hitchcock recommends.

I'll concede that *Saboteur* isn't likely to make anyone's short list of Alfred Hitchcock's greatest films. It's not as nerve-jangling as *Rear Window*, not as engrossing as *Vertigo*, not as groundbreaking as *Psycho*. It lacks the superb performances which illuminated *Shadow of a Doubt* and *Notorious* and the lavish production values which graced *To Catch a Thief* and *North by Northwest*.

But if *Saboteur* doesn't belong in the canon of Hitchcock masterpieces (which also includes *Strangers on a Train* and a few others), it holds its own on a crowded second tier full of flawed but marvelously entertaining pictures (such as *Suspicion*, *Lifeboat* and many more). For its kinetic pace, thrilling set pieces and abundance of colorful supporting characters, *Saboteur* has long ranked among my personal favorite Hitchcock creations.

CREDITS: Producer: Frank Lloyd; Associate Producer: Jack H. Skirball; Director: Alfred Hitchcock (Courtesy of David O. Selznick Productions); Screenplay: Peter Viertel, Joan Harrison, Dorothy Parker; Cinematographer: Joseph Valentine; Assistant Director: Fred Frank; Editor: Otto Ludwig; Art Director: Jack Otterson; Associate: Robert Boyle; Set decorator: R.A. Gausman; Set continuity: Adele Cannon; Musical Director: Charles Previn; Score: Frank Skinner; Sound Director: Bernard B. Brown; Technician: William Hedgcock. A Universal Picture, produced and released in 1942 in black and white; Running Time: 108 minutes

CAST: Priscilla Lane (Pat); Robert Cummings (Barry); Otto Kruger (Tobin); Alan Baxter (Freeman); Clem Bevans (Neilson); Norman Lloyd (Fry); Alma Kruger (Mrs. Sutton); Vaughan Glazer (Mr. Miller); Dorothy Peterson (Mrs. Mason); Ian Wolfe (Robert); Frances Carson (Society woman); Murray Alper (Truck driver); Kathryn Adams (Young mother); Pedro DeCordova (Bones); Billy Curtis (Midget); Marie LeDeaux (Fat woman); Anita Bolster (Lorelei); Jeanne Romer and Lynn Romer (Siamese twins)

Ronald Reagan and Casablanca: Debunking the Myth
by Carl Schult

There's been a great deal of speculation in recent months which implies that actor Humphrey Bogart was given the leading role in the film *Casablanca* by virtue of the fact that Ronald Reagan either was unwilling or unable to appear in the movie. Such speculation implies that Reagan was the first and best choice for the role.

While a case can be made for such idle speculation, the notion that Ronald Reagan was the original and best choice to play the role of Rick Blaine is mostly mythical.

The facts are:

On January 7, 1942—one month after the bombing of Pearl Harbor—the Warner Bros. Hollywood News Press Service issued a release that announced that "Ann Sheridan and Ronald Reagan (would) be teamed for the third time, in *Casablanca*."

Hours later, however, Warner Bros. effectively withdrew that announcement. On January 8, the studio reported that Sheridan and Reagan had been reassigned; they would instead appear in a movie entitled *Shadow of Their Wings*.

It's important to note that Reagan did not appear in that movie, either. Eventually retitled *Wings for the Eagle*, the film featured Ann Sheridan and actor Dennis Morgan. Possibly this was due to the fact that, as a lieutenant in the United States Army Reserve—think ROTC—Reagan's commission had been activated.

To phrase this more forcefully, Ronald Reagan had been drafted into the Army, for active service in World War II.

On February 12, 1942, Warner Bros. Executive Producer Hal B. Wallis told fellow studio producers, in a memo, to "please figure on Humphrey Bogart and Ann Sheridan for *Casablanca*." Wallis would later claim that, military service or not, Ronald Reagan was not exactly the ideal choice for the lead role in *Casablanca*; he would further assert that he (Wallis) had been thinking of Bogart for the *Casablanca* role from the start. And despite a last-minute effort by the notoriously self-important actor George Raft to secure the role for himself, Raft—who had effectively made Bogart a rising-star-by-default by turning down the roles eventually played by Bogart in the films *High Sierra* and *The Maltese Falcon*—was politely rebuffed by Wallis and studio head Jack Warner, thereby securing Bogart's lasting place in movie history.

In any event, Reagan—then an ardent Democrat—missed out on two scores: He wasn't cast in *Casablanca* and, as a soldier, the only shooting he was associated with for the duration of the war was shooting Army instructional films and propaganda-oriented short subjects... mostly on the Warner Bros. back lot, in Hollywood, USA.

In truth, the only tangible evidence that Reagan had ever even been associated with the role of Rick Blaine in the movie *Casablanca* remains the original January 7, 1942 press release... that was retracted almost instantly.

The character in *Casablanca* originally intended for Ann Sheridan was named Lois Meredith. That character was rewritten extensively; what remains of the Lois Meredith part appears in *Casablanca* as Yvonne—played by actress Madeleine LeBeau—indelicately rejected by Rick Blaine (Bogart), and eventually turning up at Rick's Café Americaine on the arm of a Nazi soldier.

The female lead in *Casablanca* was rewritten entirely, and given the name Ilsa Lund.

Interestingly, the highest-paid actor on the *Casablanca* set was Conrad Veidt, in the supporting role of German Major Heinrich Strasser. A recent refugee from Nazi persecution in his native Austria, Veidt—on loan from MGM—had been a relative bargain for Warner Bros. at a price of $25,000 for five weeks' work; 20th Century-Fox had required $7,000 per week for his primary competition, actor Otto Preminger. Most of the other cast members, including Bogart and Paul Henried (cast in the role of Victor Laszlo), were Warner Bros. contract players, meaning that they earned exactly the same salaries performing in *Casablanca* as they did for every other movie they made, year-round (Bogart had performed in some 34 Warner Bros. features since signing his contract; desperate to recreate his Broadway success as Duke Mantee in the film version of *The Petrified Forest*, he had signed his studio contract in 1936. If you're not aware of how [un]fairly Hollywood studios of that era negotiated contracts under such circumstances, just ask the heirs of Bela Lugosi). Swedish actress Ingrid Bergman, cast as Ilsa Lund, was under exclusive contract to independent producer David O. Selznick. Warner Bros. paid any recompense for her services directly to Selznick International Pictures, from which Bergman drew her regular weekly salary.

We can't imagine anyone other than Ingrid Bergman and Humphrey Bogart starring in *Casablanca*.

And, to be sure, at that point there was little or no reason to believe that *Casablanca* was anything special. It was the rule rather than the exception that the actors would arrive on the set in the morning to act in scenes written the night before—or even later, on the set. The July 17, 1942 filming of the

Bogart and Sydney Greenstreet trade barbs in *Casablanca*.

Claude Rains and Bogart: The start of a beautiful friendship

movie's climax—the airport scene—was something of a luxury for the actors; they had actually been given most of their lines some 24 hours in advance, although additional shots were taken a few days later, mostly for coverage from different angles. The movie's final line of dialogue—the classic "beautiful friendship" line—was looped, or recorded, long after the completion of principal filming. As the character delivering that line has his back turned to the camera, the effect is impossible to notice.

But it wasn't all *Bedtime for Bonzo* for Ronald Reagan either: *Brother Rat* (also starring first wife Jane Wyman), *King's Row*, *Juke Girl* and many others are fine films; conversely, if a film fan hasn't seen Humphrey Bogart as the bad guy in cowboy movies such as *The Oklahoma Kid*, or *Virginia City* (with James Cagney and Errol Flynn as the good guys, respectively), or—for God's sake—as a vampiric fiend in *The Return of Dr. X*...well, you've got some more movies to see, my friend.

It might also be noted that, on occasion, a film actor announces a "permanent retirement from the screen," but is lured back—sometimes years later—for a myriad of reasons: Silent movie actress Mary Pickford, once "America's Sweetheart" and the most recognized and celebrated film personality in the world, was sought after by director Billy Wilder for the Norma Desmond role in 1950's *Sun-

set Blvd.*, but talks fell through (three years earlier Pickford had actually submitted to the indignity of a screen test, for a leading role in the film version of *Life with Father*, but the producers cast Irene Dunne in the role instead); Cary Grant had for some time held an option on playing the Frank Galvin character in *The Verdict*, a part eventually played in 1982 by Paul Newman; Princess Grace (Kelly) of Monaco was in active negotiations to return to movies on more than one occasion, most notably for one more film with director Alfred Hitchcock; and—a full two decades after his 1961 retirement—James Cagney actually was lured back, twice, for roles in *Ragtime* and the made-for-television movie *Terrible Joe Moran*.

Similarly, Academy Award–winning actresses, and 1930s icons, Claudette Colbert and Loretta Young performed in made-for television movies during the 1980s.

The title role in the 1970 movie *Patton* was written specifically for actor Robert Mitchum, then still an active member of the film community. The producers went as far as to commission a portrait of Mitchum, in full military costume as General Patton, to be used in the film, but also to make the role more attractive to the actor. But Mitchum turned the portrait, and the movie, down flat... for no other reason than stating that acting the role was more strenuous an effort than he was willing to make, or ever would make again. And it was Mitchum who insisted that the role instead be offered to actor George C. Scott.

While it cannot be accurately reported that he actively campaigned for the role of General Patton, Ronald Reagan—by then better-known as the popular, and politically conservative, Republican governor of California—reportedly made it clear to *Patton*'s producers that he was available to be lured back before the cameras, with the right offer.

But, again, Ronald Reagan's participation in the project was politely, and quietly, declined. While certainly popular with audiences during his film career, a B-movie actor he was, and a B-movie actor Ronald Reagan would remain.

Robert Lees (1912-2004) A Tribute
by Jeff Miller

Robert Lees, along with writing partner Fred Rinaldo, crafted some of Abbott and Costello's greatest flicks, including my personal favorite, *Abbott and Costello Meet Frankenstein*. In fact, that movie so impressed me that I eventually wrote the book *The Horror Spoofs of Abbott and Costello* to celebrate those fantastic and entertaining comedies. I knew Mr. Lees and interviewed him twice, once for *Filmfax* magazine and once on stage at the Alex Theater where we introduced a special screening of *A&C Meet Frankenstein* one Halloween season. He

Screenwriter Robert Lees, left, actor John Randolph, center, and screenwriter Bernard Gordon, three blacklisted men who denounced the lifetime achievement Oscar to director Elia Kazan, in March 1999

was a charming and gentle man with a twinkle in his eye and told many great stories about his life in Hollywood. His experiences being blacklisted during the McCarthy era had not left him bitter; rather he spoke candidly about the period and was always willing to take time to educate fans (myself included) on what really happened during those infamous times. All this makes his horrifying recent murder, on June 13, 2004 at the age of 91, even more shocking. A homeless man was arrested but police had no motive for the murder of Lees and his next-door neighbor.

No one deserves that kind of brutal fate, especially one who has brought so much enjoyment to the world. Because of this, I felt it was my duty—and my honor—to write a brief reminiscence of Robert Lees.

Lees was born in San Francisco in 1912. He moved to Los Angeles in the 1930s where he briefly attended UCLA. Dropping out to help his father in business, Lees eventually took extra work at MGM. He appeared in small roles in such films as *Grand Hotel* and *Rasputin and the Empress*. (He even saw newcomer Fred Astaire dance with Joan Crawford in *Dancing Lady*—"Crawford couldn't dance a lick.") Lees joined the studio's junior writing department where he met his future collaborator Fred Rinaldo, a former Dartmouth English major. "He knew how to spell and punctuate," Lees told me, "and I knew something about the motion picture industry." Lees and Rinaldo wrote shorts for MGM including Pete Smith specialties and Robert Benchley featurettes.

Lees and Rinaldo wrote their first feature *Tomorrow Never Comes*, which Lees described as *Grapes of Wrath* set in the city. But Louis B. Mayer felt it was "politically incorrect" for MGM, so the boys took it to Lucien Hubbard at Fox. Before they knew it, they were at Universal on a picture-to-picture contract assigned to work on *Buck Privates* for the up-and-coming comedy team, Abbott and Costello.

Comedy was Lees and Rinaldo's forte and they did quite a few films for Bud and Lou including *Hold That Ghost, Hit the Ice, Buck Privates Come Home, The Wistful Widow of Wagon Gap, Abbott and Costello Meet Frankenstein, Abbott and Costello Meet the Invisible Man* and *Comin' Round the Mountain*. Lees pointed out to me that ...*Meet Frankenstein* was one of the few times that Bud and Lou stuck to the script—even though they initially didn't care for it. Though Lees admired the team, especially Lou's agility doing physical comedy, he was honest about his frustration with them. To him, Lou Costello didn't know a good gag when he saw it. "He had no concept of a good picture being anything

more than Abbott and Costello. He was the ego guy…He was really a shortsighted character."

Lees and Rinaldo also wrote *Crazy House* for Olsen and Johnson and the horror comedies *The Invisible Woman* featuring John Barrymore as a loony inventor and the underrated 1941 *The Black Cat* with Broderick Crawford, Hugh Herbert and Bela Lugosi. All of these still hold up today as fun, rainy afternoon fare for fans.

Lees and Rinaldo wrote a service comedy entitled "Ready, Willing and 4F" which later became *Jumping Jacks* starring Martin and Lewis. By that time, Rinaldo was through with writing while Lees had been named at the HUAC trials and blacklisted throughout the industry. He used a front for a while, then wrote under the name "J.E. Selby." Under this pseudonym, he wrote mostly for television including episodes of *Alfred Hitchcock Presents, Lassie* and *Gilligan's Island*.

Lees cited industry ageism as the reason for eventually retiring from writing. He taught for a while (he told me he often screened the Margaret Hamilton–Lou Costello scene from *Comin' Round the Mountain* for his comedy classes) and was an active member of UCLA's PLATO Society which allowed senior citizens to further their education.

I met Mr. Lees a few years back when I was working one Saturday night at Rocket Video in Los Angeles. Lees had come in to open an account with us and rent some movies. A co-

worker, who knew I had written a book about the Abbott and Costello horror comedies, called me over and introduced me. We talked for a while and I found Mr. Lees to be a charming and pleasant man.

Later that night, I decided I would write him and ask for an interview. I did so and he responded immediately. We made plans to meet on a Sunday morning at his home where I could ask him questions about his long career. Amazingly, I found that he lived a mere four blocks from my own Hollywood apartment. When I was writing *The Horror Spoofs of Abbott and Costello*, I was looking all over town for people to interview and all along one of the team's main writers lived a stone's throw away and I did not even know it.

The interview was wonderful and I believe I still have it somewhere on tape. Lees and I discussed Abbott and Costello, Olsen and Johnson and Martin and Lewis. I also asked him about the blacklist and admitted that I had little knowledge on the subject. He took the time to tell me the entire story from the beginning and I became so enraptured by his storytelling (he still had it in him) that I did not realize the tape had run out and I needed to turn it over! Thankfully, I didn't miss much and the interview ended up making a great article that was subsequently published in *Filmfax* magazine.

Afterward. I was able to present Mr. Lees with a gift. During the interview, I had asked him about the changes made in the ending of *Hold That Ghost*. Lees didn't know what I was talking about. I told him that the studio had changed the ending and put in an Andrews Sisters musical number. Lees could not believe it. He had not seen the movie since the 1940s! He asked if I could get him a copy, which I later did, and he was finally able to see the changes that had been made to his original screenplay.

A year or two later, I learned that the Alex Theater in Glendale was going to show *Abbott and Costello Meet Frankenstein* for its annual Halloween screening. I called the man in charge of programming, Randy Carter, and

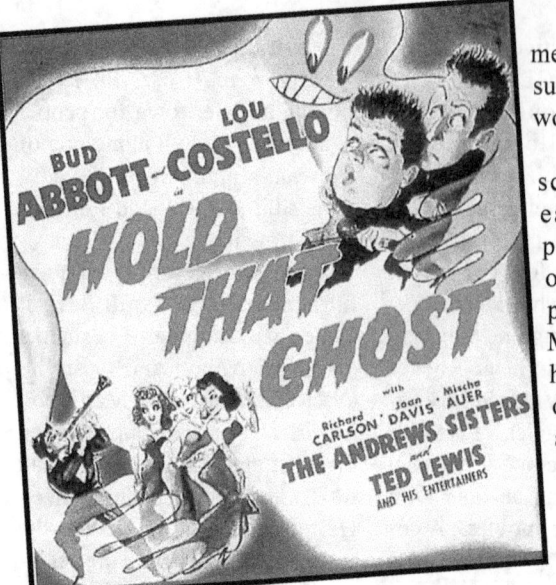

asked if I could leave some flyers at the theater promoting my book. He said I could and, as we conversed, he asked me if I knew Robert Lees as he had read an interview with the man in *Filmfax*. I told him that not only did I know Mr. Lees, but also I was the author of the article and had conducted the interview. Carter told me he was hoping to get Lees on stage for an interview before the screenings and asked me if I would like to introduce the movie and interview Lees.

Of course, I accepted. How many times do you get a chance to introduce your favorite film to a packed house of fellow fans and buffs, and interview one of your heroes at the same time?

Before going on stage, I met my friend Andrew in the men's room for a belt of courage—a shot of whiskey from a flask. I was nervous about appearing before so many people and even more nervous about being in charge of that dreaded dragon—the question and answer session. Mr. Lees came out of one of the stalls just as I was swallowing my warm taste of courage. I meekly offered him a sip. He just laughed and patted me on the back, assuring me that we would do fine.

The film was screened twice, each time to a packed house of over 1,000 people. I interviewed Mr. Lees, asking him about three or four questions about the making of the film. I remember that Lou Costello's daughter Paddy was in the audience but this didn't stop Mr. Lees from telling the crowd that he thought Lou didn't know a good gag when he saw one. Our appearances were well received and as we were going to our seats after the second intro, Lees shook my hand and said, "We did it, kid." It was one of the best experiences of my life.

From personal knowledge I can tell you that Robert Lees was a genuinely nice man. Through his film and television work he brought enjoyment and laughter to the world, joyful entertainment that will continue to delight generations to come. I would love to think that he is in a better place, joining the classic comedy teams and still writing hilarious hi-jinks for them. He will be missed.

THE SHERLOCK HOLMES
COLLECTON: VOLUME ONE
Sherlock Holmes
and the Voice of Terror: 2.5
Sherlock Holmes
and the Secret Weapon: 2.5
Sherlock Holmes
in Washington: 3.0
Sherlock Holmes
Faces Death: 3.0
Disc: 4.0
[MPI Home Video]

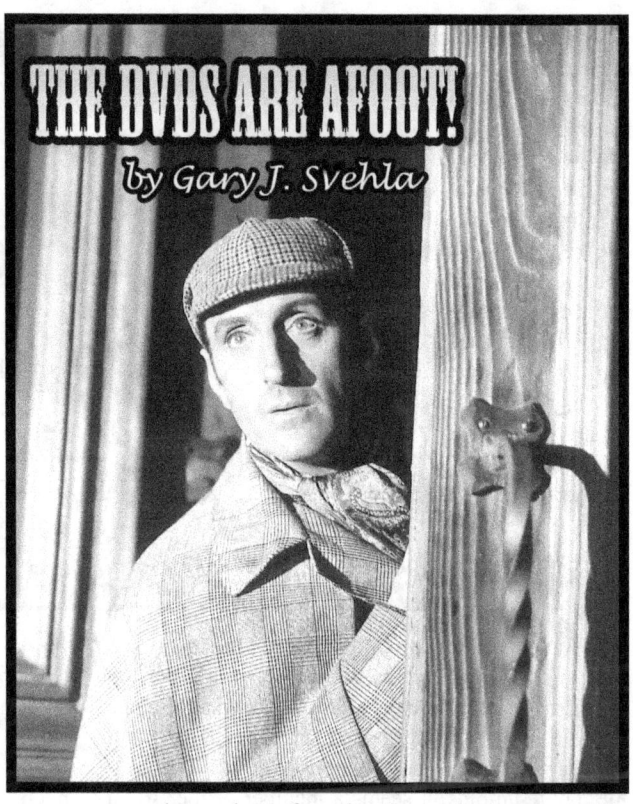

THE DVDS ARE AFOOT!
by Gary J. Svehla

After 20th Century-Fox's two A productions of *The Adventures of Sherlock Holmes* and *Hound of the Baskervilles* in 1939, the movie franchise moved to Universal and was rekindled downward from A to B productions. So much the better. At Universal the B movie became an art form in the early to mid-1940s, giving a second life to the classic Universal horrors in tremendously successful Monster Rally productions. Sherlock Holmes, in the guise of Basil Rathbone (Holmes) and Nigel Bruce (Watson), was tailor-made for the resulting B series, with scripts suggested by specific stories or overall by the works of Arthur Conan Doyle. The results were movies that cut to the chase lasting little more than an hour, featuring those wondrously moody Universal sets, foggy cinematography and casts featuring wonderful talent such as George Zucco, Lionel Atwill, Rondo Hatton, Gale Sondergaard and Evelyn Ankers. How could Universal go wrong? And MPI, working with the UCLA Film and Television Archive, has completely remastered every movie, some looking slightly better than the rest, but all of them looking and sounding the best they have in decades. For those fans who ignored the Sherlock Holmes series, now is the time to discover one of the true delights of 1940s cinema. All 12 Universal productions will be sold individually or in box sets each containing four movies. Here is a rundown of the first four movies, or the first volume box set.

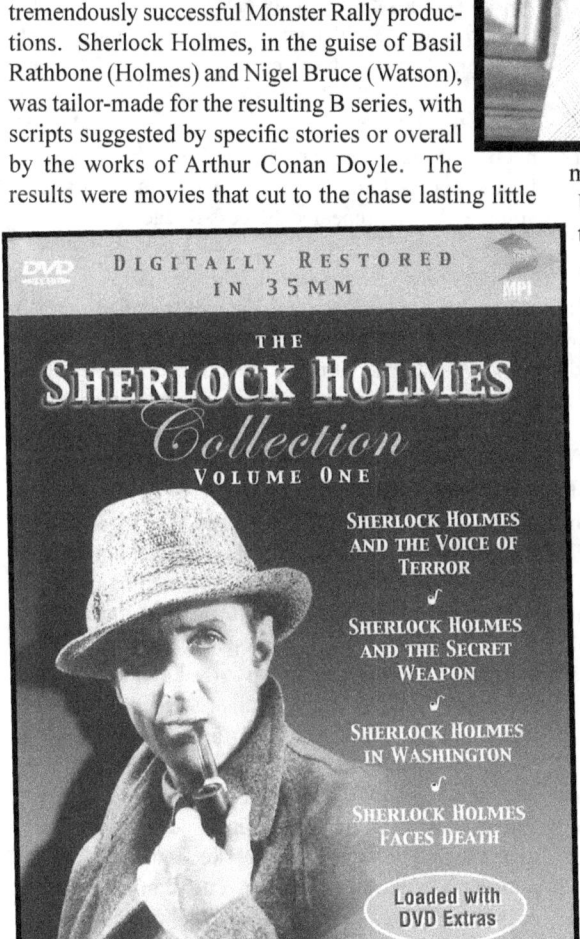

Sherlock Holmes and the Voice of Terror (1942) was a fitting introduction to the Universal series. Updating the characters of Holmes and Watson to modern times, putting them in a Nazi spy plot and forcing them to wear modern clothing (no deerstalker cap for Holmes), Holmes and Watson visit modern America but remain faithful to their classic British roots. The false note is the ridiculous hairstyle that Holmes sports in the first three entries (looking as if he were caught in a strong cross-breeze). Often times we find ourselves watching the strange hair when we should be paying more attention to the plot. Interestingly enough, the plot concerns Nazi terrorists working in Great Britain whose "Voice of Terror" announces

Mad About Movies 4

terrorist acts before they happen (trains running off the tracks, factories blowing up, etc.). Such activity parallels similar activity around the world today. Thomas Gomez portrays Nazi agent Mead who is romanced by sexy vixen Evelyn Ankers, who goes "undercover" for Holmes and the British government to capture the man who murdered her lover. For such a dirty job, she has to learn to "sleep" with the enemy, and thus Ankers forgoes her usual prim and proper persona to portray a street-wise working class woman. Gomez, both sleazy yet considerate and kind, creates a depth to his character not usually found in B productions. As the movie unfolds, it seems a member of the British Intelligence Council is a double-agent, one abetting the Nazis, and his identity only becomes known during the movie's climax. Horror veteran Henry Daniell plays one of the members of the Council, one who is simply a red herring or the double agent, as time will reveal. While *Voice of Terror* is the lesser of all four movies in this first collection, it is still a superior and thought-provoking B production that keeps audiences guessing until the end.

Sherlock Holmes and the Secret Weapon (1942) features another Nazis-infiltrate-England plot, one that is devilishly clever involving an agent who leads both Holmes and his arch-nemesis Dr. Moriarty on the trail of a secret war weapon coveted both by the Nazis and the British. Wily Lionel Atwill portrays arch-criminal mastermind Dr. Moriarty with just the right touch of affected mania and genius, one whose passion in life is one-upping the great Sherlock Holmes. Even though the Moriarty-Holmes sequences come in the last quarter of the movie, the shenanigans which lead up to the revelation of Moriarty are wonderful enough that the final quarter hour seems to leap into hyper-drive. We have a wonderful sequence with Holmes hidden in the false bottom of a crate by the villains, being rescued by Watson and the even more doddering Inspector Lestrade (Dennis Hoey). But in the film's clenched-fist climax, Moriarity and Holmes trade barbs as Holmes is strapped to a table with the good doctor threatening to drain every drop of blood from his body. However, Holmes is able to turn the tables with Moriarty stupidly falling through his own trap door that drops to the Thames river below. Any other villain would be dead from such a drop, but Moriarty always returns. In these final sequences, *The Secret Weapon* comes dangerously close to becoming a mad lab horror movie with Rathbone becoming the ultimate gentleman hero to Atwill's equally distinguished villain. Roy William Neill's debut as director of the series (he would direct this and every other entry and produce all but one of them) was a masterstroke, as his sensitivity for the material and for the suspense quotient speaks volumes for the repeated success of each entry in the series.

Sherlock Holmes in Washington (1943) is generally underrated as just another workmanlike entry in the Holmes series, but out of these first four entries, *In Washington* is definitely the best. Generally, these early Sherlock Holmes movies all end with Holmes delivering some propaganda message, and Holmes' visit to the States is ample excuse to wave the flag on our behalf. But the mystery and plotting, even the plot gimmicks, are wonderfully inspired. The film starts out aboard a train as Nazi spy Henry Daniell and cohorts try to identify a decoy British agent, whom they figure out is the meek character portrayed by Gerald Hamer. When he senses the Nazis are on to him, he has minutes to hide the microfilm he is carrying. Drinks are shared, cigarettes are lighted and small articles are passed between people. As it turns out, the microfilm is glued in-between the split matchbook cover that has been passed on to a young lady traveling aboard the train. When Hamer's character is kidnapped and thrown into a car, the female (Marjorie Lord) keeps the matches and puts them in her purse. During one of many climaxes of the movie, in a sequence very Hitchcockian in tone, during a party, the viewer gets to watch as the book of matches gets passed around between people, ends up on a silver platter and finally makes its way back into the lady's purse. Very clever, very suspenseful and quite

Basil Rathbone and Lionel Atwill in *Sherlock Holmes and the Secret Weapon*

well filmed to heighten the suspense. By the film's end, Holmes traces the network of spies, who have kidnapped the woman, to an antiques dealer played by the sinister and highly effective George Zucco. At one point Zucco holds the woman's book of matches and lights up, never realizing he holds the object of his obsession right in his own hands. In a clever twist, Holmes concocts an equally devilish plot to lure Zucco to a Senator's office (who was also a passenger aboard the train) thinking he will be securing the microfilm, when in fact Holmes sets the entire meeting up so he could get his hands on the matchbook. Besides the wonderful sleight of hand aboard the train, the wonderful "who-has-the-matchbook" shell game at the party, the old "don't-turn-around" trick of having the villains get the upper hand on Holmes by appearing behind him entering from a secret passage in the wall and the final "hot potato" trade-offs in the Senator's office, *Sherlock Holmes in Washington* is one of the more enthralling entries in the entire Universal series, and it contains one of the best written scripts with the most clever twists. Even the character of Watson comes front and center with Nigel Bruce's Americanizing antics such as chewing gum and slurping down a milkshake often stealing the spotlight from Rathbone.

Finally, *Sherlock Holmes Faces Death* (1943) is almost as entertaining as *In Washington*. For the first time, the Nazi spy plotting has been dropped in favor of a Universal mood piece occurring in a spooky mansion (now being used as a rehab hospital for soldiers wounded in the war) where a fiendish murderer strikes. *Faces Death* is based upon the short story

The Adventure of the Musgrave Ritual, and the setting of the ancient mansion makes this adventure seem less contemporary and more the period piece. And for the first time since the ending of *Secret Weapon*, this Holmes entry comes very close to approximating the tone of Universal's Old Dark House mysteries. During the conclusion, the Musgrave Ritual is played out, quite clever visually, as a giant chess game played upon a checker-board floor. But the grisly plot follows the murder of the two Musgrave males—both are stabbed in the neck—after the first attempt to knock off the family physician fails. Lovely Hillary Brooke is the last Musgrave to be taken care of, allowing the murderer to acquire the family fortune. Literally taking the title of the movie quite seriously, during the climax, Sherlock Holmes and the family doctor are alone in the cellar, with Holmes protecting a message, written in the blood of a recent murder victim (the family butler) as he lay dying. When the doctor reaches for the cloth covering the message, Holmes' hand reaches out and grabs the wrist of the doctor, stating there was no message. It was just a clever plot employed by Holmes to lure the killer back to the murder scene. Acting quite stupidly, Holmes, holding a pistol on the doctor, allows the doctor to come too close and overpower him; the doctor now points the weapon at Holmes. Then in proud restatement of how he committed the murders, the doctor fires several shots point blank into the shocked Holmes, who falls to the wall apparently mortally wounded. Of course, the pistol was filled with blanks and Holmes needed the murderer to make a complete confession, overheard by authorities above, later revealing that egomaniacs always have to boast of their deeds, something Holmes was counting on to prove the guilt of the doctor (who, insidiously, used a needle inserted into the brains to kill his victims, not the decoy knife in the neck that gained the immediate attention). *Sherlock Holmes Faces Death* is the first Gothic entry in the series, and fittingly, it is the first one where Holmes sports more distinguished hair styling. Sherlock Holmes finds himself in a frightening mansion with a serial killer on the loose—what better opportunity for Universal to demonstrate its strengths by blending mystery and horror in one suspenseful mystery chiller?

1. OPEN
2. MUSGRAVE MANOR
3. DOCTOR IN THE HOUSE
4. "A KILLER LOOSE!"
5. EXTRAORDINARY PATIENTS
6. "THAT APPALLING MAN FROM SCOTLAND YARD"
7. THE MUSGRAVE RITUAL
8. THE RAT AND THE RAVEN
9. THE BUTLER DID IT?
10. THE RITUAL SOLVED
11. CHECKMATE
12. END CREDITS

Extras in this beautiful boxed set include a 16-page illustrated book with liner notes by Richard Valley, audio commentary by David Stuart Davies, photo galleries and poster galleries. But most important is the remastering of the original 35mm source material to a level not seen since the 1940s. These first four Sherlock Holmes Universal adventures have been overlooked for far too long, and their resurfacing here is cause for celebration. I cannot wait to dig into the second box set and revisit the next four entries.

THE SHERLOCK HOLMES COLLECTION: VOLUME TWO
The Pearl of Death: 2.5
The Scarlet Claw: 3.0
The Spider Woman: 2.5
The House of Fear: 3.0
Disc: 4.0
[MPI Home Video]

Surprisingly, I always thought the Universal horror-themed Sherlock Homes entries were the pick of the litter, the absolute peak of artistic form where Universal could merge its horror character actors (Gale Sondergaard, Rondo Hatton, Evelyn Ankers, Lionel Atwill, etc.), its moody Gothic sets with the classic mystery genre to produce the finest of the B Sherlock Holmes productions. But quite surprisingly, the first four entries, all but one dealing with the Nazis and World War II, all quite compelling, turned out to be much better than I remembered. Lionel Atwill's turn as Moriarity and the exciting climax of *Secret Weapon* and the Hitchcock-influenced *In Washington* become two delights with wit and intelligence in both characterization and plot construction. The first Gothic chiller, *Faces Death*, became another classic Old Dark House mystery where Universal's horror sets and moody, misty photography came to the forefront.

With volume, two MPI presents the overall most popular entries in the series, but with fresh eyes and gorgeous new prints, let's see how these entries hold up when compared to the earlier movies.

First up is *The Pearl of Death*, based upon Doyle's short story *The Six Napoleons*, and featuring a trio of villainy portrayed by Evelyn Ankers (Naomi Drake), Miles Mander (the Moriarty-like Giles Conover) and Rondo Hatton (the Hoxton Creeper). The film, which lags in the middle, starts off quite wonderfully with two classic sequences. The first, occurring during a vacation cruise, shows how the wily Naomi lures a gentleman housing the museum quality Borgia Pearl (a monster of a pearl) away from his cabin, where the pearl, to be delivered to a British museum, is hidden in a secret compartment in his luggage. Naomi, working quickly, knows just where to find the pearl, but suspecting a customs investigation, asks a kindly elderly reverend to hold the pearl for her. He hesitates at first, but soon politely agrees. Of course as it turns out the elderly clergyman is none other than a disguised Sherlock Holmes, and when Naomi reports to her boss, the evil mastermind Giles Conover, she delivers a note signed by Holmes telling the duo they have been tricked.

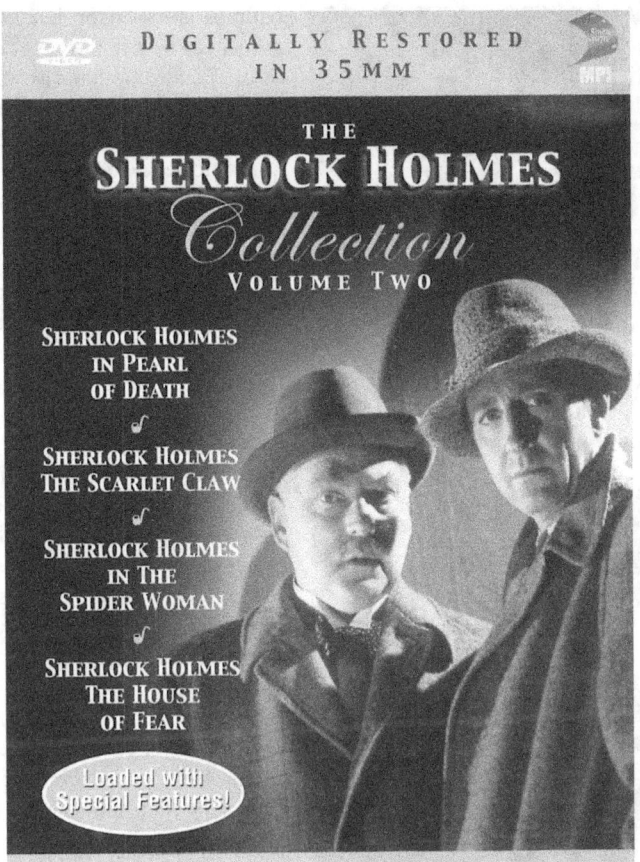

Canover, working undercover as a maintenance main in the very museum where the Borgia Pearl will be housed, has his ear against the wall when the wily Holmes disconnects the museum's security system, he making the case that the security system, dependent upon four wires, is grossly inadequate. During Holmes' demonstration, when the security system is turned off, Conover makes a play to steal the pearl and escapes by crashing through a glass window to the outside. Even though he allows himself to be captured almost immediately, he has had time to hide the pearl.

Soon murders begin to occur, with the victims dying of a broken spine cracked at the third lumbar vertebrae.

Rathbone and Nigel Bruce pose for a publicity shot for *The Pearl of Death*.

And at the murder scene various statues and curios lie shattered near the corpse. Of course Rondo Hatton's Creeper is the monstrous tool of Conover who has hid the Borgia Pearl inside one of six busts of Napoleon, and one by one, he sends the Creeper out to retrieve the bust, smash it, and to return the pearl if he finds it inside. It is exactly this middle third of the film that becomes strangely lethargic; lots of time spent on the ineffectiveness of Dennis Hoey's Lestrade, whose participation in this production is long and tedious. The final murder occurs and Holmes assumes yet another disguise as the film's climax comes to its spine tingling and dramatic conclusion. Seldom has the here-voiceless Creeper character been used so effectively, his hulking, lumbering figure wearing a bowler hat contrasted to the petite and also lumbering Conover, who wears exactly the same type of hat. Thus this shadowy duo becomes quite menacing and Rondo Hatton would never appear quite as all-powerfully monstrous ever again. Roy William Neill's direction shines in such sequences and proves him to be a true master of the horror-mystery genre.

The Scarlet Claw, released in 1944, is considered

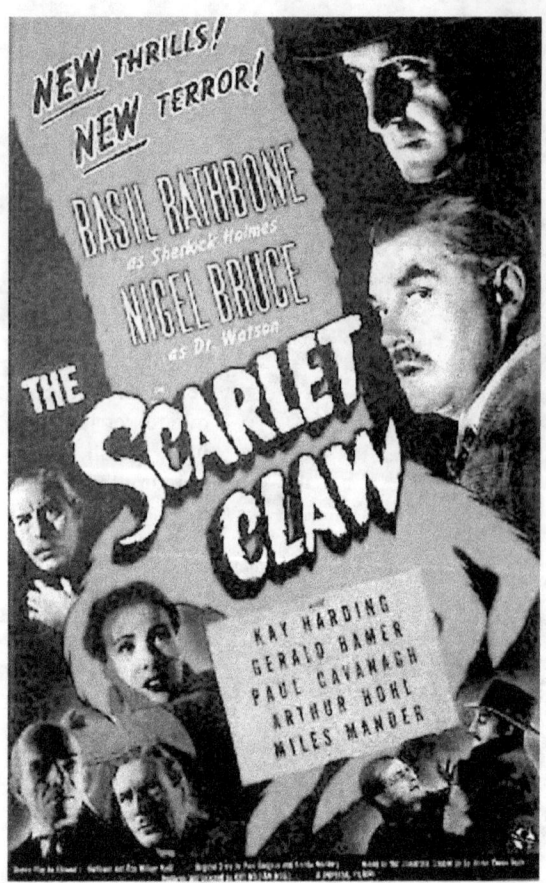

as one contender for best in series, and it very well might be. Talk about the perfect blending of Holmes, mystery and Universal horror, the first five minutes of *The Scarlet Claw* drips with the mood of classic horror. In a rural Canadian tavern, the local citizenry gather to discuss, with their parish priest, grisly murders of farm animals and the apparent return of La Morte Rouge, a marsh fiend of legendary proportions. In the midst of this interior camp-side ghost story, the clanging of the church bells is heard, as Lady Penrose, savagely attacked in the marshes, musters strength to ring the bell for help before she dies, her throat torn out. Meanwhile at a meeting of the Royal Canadian Occult Society, Lord Penrose (Paul Cavanagh) debates matters of the occult with skeptic Sherlock Holmes, when Penrose is abruptly called away due to the sudden death of his wife. Sherlock Holmes and Watson are involved in this case because Holmes receives a letter from Lady Penrose stating she believed her life was in danger and asking the assistance of Holmes.

A *Hound of the Baskervilles*-inspired sequence, out on the moors, where a phosphorous specter attacks

A disguised Holmes baits Watson before explaining he's not dead yet in *The Spider Woman*.

Holmes and Watson becomes one of the moodiest sequences ever in the Universal horror canon. A scrap of the fiend's clothing is found on a tree branch and Holmes deduces that an ordinary human being is wearing glow-in-the-dark costuming—that the legend of Le Morte Rouge is simply that… myth. It turns out that Lady Penrose, a former actress, was a member of the same theatrical troupe as current killer Alastair Ramson, who is a master of disguise. In one spectacular sequence, Holmes and Watson approach the home of a reclusive judge (Miles Mander, for once playing a victim and not an ace criminal) in the dead of night to warn him his life is in great danger. As the duo knock on his door, Holmes can literally see the judge seated at his desk while his housekeeper Nora attends to his needs. However, when an unusual delay occurs in answering the door, Holmes breaks inside to find the judge dead with his throat ripped out (the murder tool is a five-pronged garden trowel); Ramson had disguised himself as the judge's female house servant. The suspense of such a sequence is high-octane, simply because Holmes arrives at the judge's home and sees the elderly man safely snuggled in his study, the ace detective is able to take a deep breath thinking he arrived in plenty of time to save the judge's life. Even more savage, a young female teenager is surprisingly murdered in a similar fashion by Ramson when the killer's identity is almost revealed.

During the film's climax, the killer escapes to freedom by jumping through a window into the harbor waters below. It is a wonderfully moody sequence that features a fabulous stunt escape. But all the red-herrings are eliminated when it turns out that the seemingly harmless postman Potter turns out to be the fiend, ready to attack Holmes with his garden trowel. But the clever Holmes is already waiting for the attempt on his life.

The Scarlet Claw shines by virtue of its interesting characterizations and Gothic setting, its elusive and multi-disguised fiend, an interesting script that actually makes the mystery one of the best of the series and perhaps features the finest cinematography in the entire series. *The Scarlet Claw* is absolutely perfect on every level, and the film's pacing, nail-biting script and wonderful performances by Rathbone and Bruce (yes, Watson is not the doddering fool he has been painted to be and his performances improve with these repeated viewings) never disappoint.

Also in 1944, *The Spider Woman* was released, a Holmes entry built around a female Moriarty called The Spider Woman and played to the hilt of villainy by Gale Sondergaard, who was probably the stereotypical

Basil Rathbone poses in character for publicity shots for the Sherlock Holmes film series.

female villain of the Golden Age of Hollywood. Her performance as Adrea Spedding is simply delicious, her cold face with deceptive eyes wrapped around double-entrendre dialogue which makes her almost the equal of Holmes. And the basic plot is quite gripping, involving a series of pajama murders where men in their night clothes jump to their deaths in the dark of night. Holmes, who assumes two major disguises in this entry, first fakes his own death while on a fishing trip with Watson, apparently falling into a gushing stream and drowning. Holmes believes that Waston, in his writing, has revealed so much about his *modus operandi* that the villains are now getting the upper hand. In a tear-soaked sequence at his Baker Street residence, all of Holmes' goods are being boxed and carted off to the British museum; even Inspector Lestrade is emotionally wrecked and yells at Watson for failing to jump into the water to save his friend. However, shortly thereafter, a disguised Holmes returns to his home and surprises Watson, who nearly collapses.

Holmes' major disguise is an Indian military officer who gambles and loses big, becoming acquainted with Adrea Spedding who tries to blow a little luck on the roulette wheel. When the despondent Indian is on the verge of committing suicide with a small pistol, Adrea directs him to her friend who will give him cash if he makes this friend the beneficiary of his large insurance policy. Of course in the follow-up sequence at Adrea's home, the sharp dialogue hints that Holmes knows that Adrea is the black widow killer, while Adrea implies she recognizes the disguise and knows she is in the company of Holmes, even going so far as to spill hot tea on his paralyzed arm to prove he has movement. Later that evening a deadly spider crawls through the vent of the Indian's bedroom ready to strike the sleeping victim when the actual Holmes jumps out to reveal the sleeping body is only a dummy, as he skewers the spider with his knife.

The film's climax occurs at a carnival where Adrea and her henchman operate, using a pygmy (actually little person Angelo Rossitto in blackface, no less) hidden in a suitcase to deliver the spider to its destination. Here Holmes is outsmarted and surprised and tied to the back of an arcade target-shooting contest, the metal plate removed from Hilter's heart so the rifle bullet will instead penetrate Holmes' heart instead. Of course crack shot Watson is the man who is taking dead aim at Hilter, but his distractions allow Holmes time to cut through the ropes that bind him and thus allow him to apprehend the criminal gang, with Lestrade's

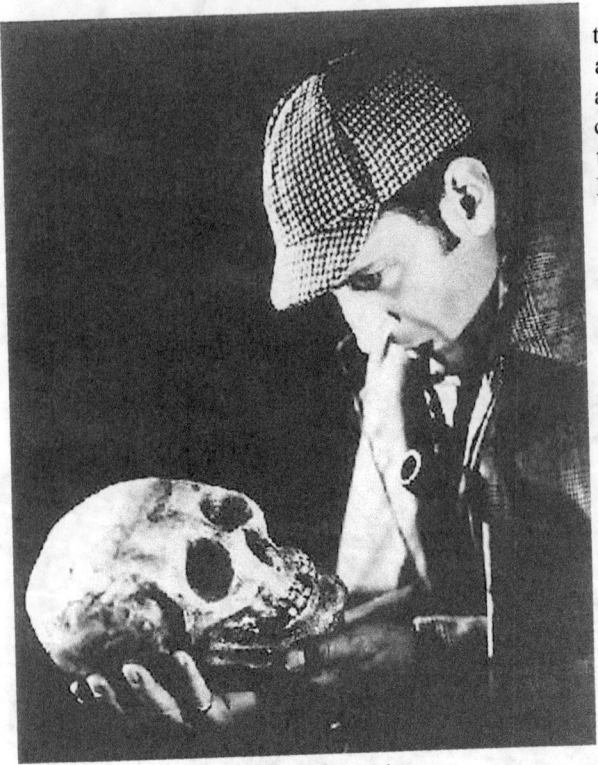
Alas poor Yorick!

that also populated Universal's *Son of Frankenstein* and *Bride of Frankenstein*. Here the major set pieces are ancient Gothic, but there are hints of modern conveniences (such as a car or two) reminding us that the setting is a contemporary one… even if Dreacliff House does not have telephones.

Clues to the ultimate mystery are given early on when the bodies of the dead are mutilated, suggesting right from the start that the murderer may have planned his own death (usually another body, of course) to throw suspicion from him. However, when almost all of the bodies are unidentified, the only corpse able to be identified is the seaman who had a tattoo on his chest. By the end of the movie an even stranger secret is revealed, one that is now a chestnut of the mystery genre but was quite startling and original at the time of the story's publication. The mystery element is always suspensefully handled and intriguing, and Rathbone and Bruce's contributions are always interesting and integral to the plot. But *The House of Fear* shines brightest because of the carefully woven plot that features victims/red-herrings that are carefully constructed and emerge as involving characters that hold our interest. The gloomy mansion, the huge dining room table, the smuggler's cave and beach setting all contribute to the ambience and aura of dread. While *The House of Fear* features that generic Universal title, the movie itself is one of the better Holmes entries and becomes anything but generic.

Once again *Volume Two* contains Robert Gitt's introduction explaining how the Holmes movies were restored and the challenges his team faced, some audio commentaries by David Stuart Davies, original poster and still gallery and liner notes by Richard Valley. I never realized just how much I would enjoy seeing these four Sherlock Homes Universal mysteries, but after Volume One and Two, I can hardly wait for the final four films to arrive shortly in Volume Three. These 12 films are a welcome delight and one of the more entertaining DVD releases of the past year.

help. Surprisingly, Holmes asks the police not to cuff the Spider Woman, Holmes showing her overt respect for her criminal prowess and style in her nefarious activities. One almost gets the idea that some chemistry might actually exist between the two dueling adversaries and that Holmes realizes he may have finally met his match.

Simply stated, *The Spider Woman* is again one of the best entries, not consistently as strong as *The Scarlet Claw* and some of the others, but an entry that shines by virtue of its exceptional performance of evil and its two or three outstanding sequences.

1945's *The House of Fear* continues the Old Dark House Holmes mysteries that began with *Faces Death* and *The Scarlet Claw*. In fact, in many ways, *House of Fear* might well be the most effectively constructed mystery scenario of them all. Based upon the short story, *The Mystery of the Five Orange Pips*, *House of Fear* concerns the Society of Good Comrades, wealthy retirees who meet regularly to share their spirit of camaraderie. However, the club members have been dwindling in number, having been murdered one by one, each man receiving a sealed envelope with a specific number of orange pips inside, thus sealing the receiver's fate. This story influenced other similar stories such as *And Then There Were None/Ten Little Indians* and countless other similar mysteries. The action occurs at the ancestral home, Dreacliff House, of one of the founding members, and in that mythical ageless world

**THE SHERLOCK HOLMES COLLECTION:
VOLUME THREE**
The Woman in Green: 2.5
Pursuit to Algiers: 3.0
Terror by Night: 2.5
Dressed to Kill: 2.5
Disc: 4.0
[MPI Home Video]

The final four Sherlock Holmes mysteries, all released either in 1945 or 1946, are generally the most ignored of the series, entries that are always labeled as being inferior to the earlier eight entries. And while for the most part such a claim might be correct, the truth is that these final entries are perhaps at most only a half rung below some of the best (and some are better than the worst of the initial eight). Since we are speaking about B productions, programmers lasting little over an hour, it is indeed the appeal of the series, the appeal of the repartee between Rathbone and Bruce, that brings us back for more. It is always entertaining to see the economically designed yet effectively crafted sets, but the movies rise or fall upon their eccentric character studies of Holmes and Watson and the degree of mystery and of an effectively crafted story that requires Holmes and Watson to actually apply detective skills and deductive reasoning. All of these movies have merit, but some simply rise above the rest. But the true pleasure of seeing this MPI collection in its entirety is seeing the entire series from start to finish, perhaps to be enjoyed over the course of a month or two. It's the series programmer appeal that makes these low-budget productions shine, because the craftsmanship and care afforded each movie makes each entry stand out as superior B productons.

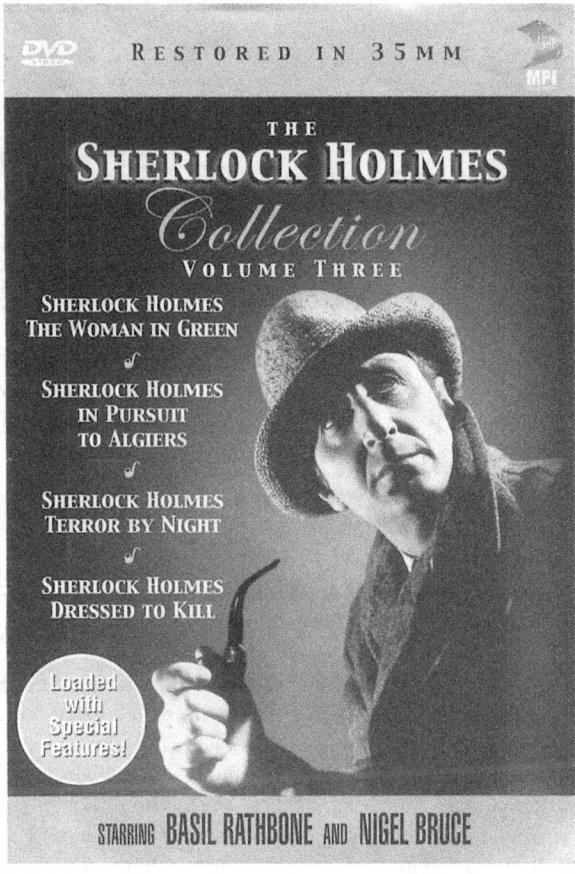

The Woman in Green (1945), although directed by Roy William Neill and featuring the recurring B cast from earlier entries (Hillary Brooke, Paul Cavanagh and Henry Daniel), seems different in flavor (and set design) from other entries, and Holmes and Watson seem to have less to do, although they are featured prominently throughout. The movie seems more like a variation on the Jack the Ripper murders with a fog-shrouded London harboring the dreaded Finger Murderer, whose female victims always have their index finger cut off and collected. *The Woman in Green*, like the immediate two movies that came before, *The Scarlet Claw* and *The Pearl of Death*, continues the trend of the recent series to feature horror motifs, in this case a mutilating fiend who preys upon women. For the third time in the series, Professor Moriarty returns, but in this case as a much inferior characterization as enacted by Henry Daniel. While Daniel exudes quiet menace in a subtle and controlled fashion, he simply lacks the panache of George Zucco (whose piercing eyes and slightly askew face mirror the insanity lurking below the grandfatherly exterior) or of Lionel Atwill, whose Moriarty is quirky, perverse and devilishly energetic. Daniel lacks even the personality and eccentricity of a Giles Conover (Miles Mander), who would have made a superior Moriarty to Daniel's interpretation. However, Hillary Brooke as the woman in green of the title, Lydia, suggests a domesticated variation of Gale Sondergaard's Spider Woman, becoming the true villain of the picture. She, who woos and then hypnotizes her victims to become killing machines, raises goose-bumps at every opportunity. The movie shines in the first third when Paul Cavanagh's distinguished gentleman, dating Lydia and coming under her spell, awakens in a tenement building, with a total mental blackout of what transpired during the last 12 hours, and when he reaches into his coat pocket he finds a dismembered finger (the audience never sees it, but we know exactly what he is feeling by his terrified expression). Cavanagh's character now believes he is the Finger Murderer, and going home, he is quickly murdered, although in death he does offer a final clue to the identity of the true fiend. The movie meanders until the final roof-top climax, where Holmes, hypnotized, walks upon the thin building ledge ready to plummet to his death below. In a sudden twist, it is revealed that Holmes is only feigning to be hypnotized and that Moriarty, attempting to escape by jumping between buildings, grabs a drain which pulls from the building, resulting in his falling to his death several stories below. Unfortunately the always delightful Dennis Hoey (Inspector Lestrade) was replaced by Matthew Boulton's Inspector Gregson, a generally colorless portrayal. While *The Woman in Green* is never bad, it is inferior (in both story and characterizations) to other entries and the plot seems to require Rathbone and Bruce to play a less important role in solving the crimes.

Pursuit to Algiers, also released in 1945, fares considerably better with a plot that features more twists, keeping its audience always guessing. The bulk of the production occurs on board a low-budget cruise ship with its claustrophobic sense that even Holmes and Watson are never safe, not even in their private cabin (which features a porthole opening on deck, thus giving criminals an opportunity to spy and to gain access to their quarters). The plot, a quite clever one, involves the death of a king and the protection of an adult-age young prince, who must be safety delivered to sympathetic countrymen in Algiers. The initial plan is for Holmes, Watson, the prince and his supporters to fly to Algiers; however, the original plane is strangely in need of repair at the last minute (something that tips off Holmes that the game's afoot) and the replacement plane cannot carry Watson, so Holmes has his dear friend book a cruise and they will meet and vacation on the other end of the voyage. Watson, always comfortable flying solo, becomes friendly with many people aboard the cruise ship until he hears of Holmes' airplane crashing into the Pyrenees. Once again, in stiff upper lip fashion, actor Nigel Bruce allows his Watson to mourn the death of his lifelong friend in such a way that the audience feels his affection and pain although the sequences are never allowed to become maudlin or sappy. In such sequences Nigel Bruce commits a subtle and compassionate portrayal, cementing once and for all the masterful performance that he seldom gets credit for delivering. Of course, almost cruelly, the always smirking Holmes ultimately shows up in perfect health and explains that he was never on the plane, that the prince is with him and will pose as Watson's nephew (but by movie's end, the audience is tricked again with the knowledge that the actual prince is the ship's steward and that the so-called nephew is simply a decoy). So as stated earlier, the plot explodes with surprises and twists.

On this ship of fools red herrings abound, and even a walk on the deck ultimately becomes ominous, especially when Holmes and Watson become involved with a shrewd jewel thief who keeps the stolen gems clutched

Watson and Holmes are surrounded by suspects in *Pursuit to Algiers*.

to her body. But this subplot is really insignificant because the real plot involves the mysterious strangers who board the cruise ship mid-voyage (one of whom is Universal perennial villain Martin Kosleck) and are there to kill the prince. In one wonderful sequence nasty villain Kosleck, the master of throwing knives, is ready to throw the deadly weapon at the prince through the porthole window, when Holmes, cleverly anticipating the dastardly attack, closes the window on Kosleck's wrist, breaking a bone and rendering Kosleck's talent useless the remainder of the movie. Another surprise awaits as an explosive is housed inside a party favor meant to be opened by the prince, but Holmes once again cleverly intercepts the fatal favor and flaunts it in front of the three assassins before he flings it into the sea. Such sequences are both thrilling and funny, fostering the notion that humor often heightens suspense and makes the generally aloof Holmes more warm and fuzzy. Featuring wonderful performances by the leads, great supports from the villains and a wonderful blending of suspense and fun, *Pursuit to Algiers* once again proves the Sherlock Holmes series is one well worth revisiting.

Sherlock Holmes and Dr. Watson would once again pack their traveliing valises for their next entry, *Terror by Night*, which used a train as the dominant set piece. The train setting allows for the claustrophobic mystery to unwind and also allows for many red herrings to be introduced in close proximity to all the action and murder. However, while *Pursuit to Algiers* was a better than average entry, *Terror by Night*, while it has its moments, is lethargic and not particularly well scripted. Professor Moriarty is dead, but the right-hand man in his criminal organization still prospers, Colonel Sebastian Moran, and he is aboard the train intending to steal the Star of Rhodesia, a priceless diamond under the watchful eye of Sherlock Holmes. The diamond is owned by the cool Lady Margaret Carstairs (Mary Forbes), and when her son is immediately murdered and the diamond found missing, the elderly Carstairs seems

Watson and Holmes fish for red herrings on a train bound for murder in *Terror by Night*.

more emotionally disturbed about the loss of the gem and not the loss of life of her son. Sebastian Moran is in disguise, posing as simply another passenger, and before long red herrings pop up everywhere. One strange lady Vivian Vedder (Renee Godfrey) accompanies the coffin of her mother, but in a false bottom of the coffin, the maniacal assassin is secretly stowed. The hit man is employed by Colonel Moran. The sniveling Cockney killer is portrayed by none other than Skelton Knaggs, one underused character actor whose other famous role was in Val Lewton's *The Ghost Ship*. Knaggs uses an air pistol to shoot poison into his victims, killing them instantly. Inspector Lestrade (Dennis Hoey), traveling along supposedly as part of a vacation, is almost a victim himself.

At the film's end, Holmes is almost killed when he is kicked off the side of the train; he just barely manages to hold on to the railing as he is under attack. Holmes reveals Colonel Moran's identity, and when Scottish police board the train to take him into custody, he becomes suspicious when Moran is not handcuffed. But Holmes is always aware of the double-cross and last-minute trickery, bringing all the intrigue and suspense to a rapid and neat conclusion. Again, while *Terror by Night* is memorable for several sequences, as a whole the movie is sometimes listless and the pacing sometimes drags. But as usual, Nigel Bruce and Basil Rathbone are perfect as Watson and Holmes, respectively.

Dressed to Kill, the final entry in the series, released in 1946, is about on par with *Terror by Night*, another script that suffers from lack of connection to the original Conan Doyle stories that helped propel earlier entries in the series. Similar to *Pearl of Death*, the plot involves a series of three simply made music boxes that carry an important coded criminal message (the boxes were produced by a criminal while in prison), and these music boxes are sold at auction before femme fatale Hilda Courtney (Patricia Morison) can acquire them. Unfortunately the film's finest moments come early on in the auction house. One of the purchasers is Stinky Emery (Edmond Breon), an old friend of Watson's. Emery, a large bandage plastered over his forehead, comes to see Watson and Holmes for help, after being attacked in his own home with one of his musical boxes stolen from his expensive collection. The repartee between Breon and Bruce is priceless, and the audience immediately warms up to the Stinky character.

Dressed to Kill marked the end for the dynamic detecting duo of Nigel Bruce and Basil Rathbone.

Unfortunately, Courtney and assistant/assassin Hamid (Harry Cording) realize they have the wrong box, so the sexy and dressed to the nines Courtney returns to visit Stinky to get the correct music box. In a rather nasty moment, when it is apparent that Courtney could walk right out of Stinky's home with the music box, Cording, hiding off to the side, throws a knife into Stinky's chest killing him instantly. While Patricia Morison entertains in the best Gale Sondergaard tradition, it seems the film could have been more entertaining if the Stinky/Watson relationship had been better developed with Stinky providing assistance in solving the case. However Morison and Cording, both working for gentleman criminal Colonel Cavanaugh (Frederick Worlock), become a rather interesting criminal syndicate. Morison is most interesting when she disguises herself as a charwoman and later when she appears at 221 B Baker Street and sets off a smoke bomb knowing that Watson will instinctively reach for the hidden music box which he and Holmes are harboring. When he produces the box and goes into the next room to find something to extinguish the fire, the wily female simply ducks out the door with the music box in hand. This leads to the dramatic climax where Holmes quite literally hangs by handcuffs off the ground awaiting his imminent death.

Of course, the villains will be defeated and Holmes rescued, but unfortunately, neither Bruce nor Rathbone would ever appear onscreen as these beloved characters again.

This third volume box set features four entries that are not as strong as the first two; however, even the weaker films of the series are of interest, and the entire set, taken as a whole, is gripping and filled with fun. The remastering of the 35mm source material (with occasional 16mm replacement footage used) is exceptional and these films can once again be seen in the manner originally intended. I rated all 12 entries as being fair to good, but for B productions that have not been overexposed, revisiting a Universal mystery series produced during the 1940s is always very special. Simply seeing those sets, that cinematography, those supporting actors and actresses and the rich interpretations given Doyle's classic characters by Nigel Bruce and Basil Rathbone make for thoroughly satisfying entertainment. Don't shortchange yourself and only buy those entries you think you'll like the most, because every volume has one or two absolute gems, many of them awaiting rediscovery. Even now, having seen all 12 entries, I am ready to dig right back into *Volume One* all over again!

Mad About Movies DVD Reviews

by Gary J. Svehla

Ratings:
4: Excellent; 3: Good;
2: Fair; 1: Poor

The Complete Monterey Pop Festival
Movie: 3.0; Disc: 4.0
[The Criterion Collection]

When it comes to the hippie era of rock 'n' roll of the late 1960s and early 1970s, most people consider Woodstock to be the ultimate historical rock document of the era. However, *Woodstock* (the movie) had the budget, the talent (even Martin Scorsese was involved) and the media hype making it both an historic as well as a cultural event of its time. For me, *The Monterey Pop Festival*, both low budget and lo-fi, has always been my favorite. Both *Woodstock* feature films offer more music and complete musical sets, but Monterey somehow seems ultimately more innocent and more culturally important, having occurred a full year before Woodstock, just as the hippie movement was being born. Director and *cinema verite* documenter D.A. Pennebaker, most renowned for his landmark documentary of Bob Dylan's 1965 tour of England, *Don't Look Back*, is here recording another type of cultural event. Monterey was not hyped or held to be culturally important, it was merely a huge rock concert and nothing more.

Pennebaker created the original *Monterey Pop* documentary, clocking in at 79 minutes, with the intention of including one song from every band, offering a pop sampler. However, when Pennebaker and crew started filming Jimi Hendrix and The Who, they threw all plans to the wind and tried to capture as much as possible. With the rush to assemble the feature, and with all the extra footage stored away, lost or simply discarded because the quality of what was filmed simply did not make the grade, what was released to theaters back in 1968 was considered complete. But Criterion approached director Pennebaker about assembling outtakes, unused footage and recreating the ultimate documentation of this pivotal concert, and this three-disc DVD set is the result. We have the original feature film, but now we have a second disc that assembles all the footage available during the musical sets of both Otis Redding (19 minutes) and Jimi Hendrix (49 minutes), offering a more intimate look at the performances of both legends. And finally,

the ultimate disc, The Outtake Performances, runs a full 123 minutes. Most importantly, the performance by The Byrds, totally cut from the original feature, is here restored, as are additional performances by The Association, The Blues Project, Buffalo Springfield, The Electric Flag, Laura Nyro, Simon and Garfunkel, Tiny Tim, Quicksilver Messenger Service, Country Joe and the Fish, The Mamas and the Papas, Paul Butterfield Blues Band and Big Brother (with Janis Joplin). All the footage has been digitally remastered and remixed with 5.1 surround sound. Also included is a 61-page full-color program that accompanies the three individually wrapped discs.

What made *Monterey Pop* so special for me is the image of the early emerging hippie, not dyed-in-the-wool as Woodstock portrayed, but just fairly straight, innocent young people growing their hair longer, painting their faces, blowing bubbles and swaying in awe to some of the best pop music created at the end of the 1960s. For fans of the counter-culture movement, and for fans of rock music of the late 1960s, *The Complete Monterey Pop Festival* is a must-have.

The Killers (1946)
The Killers (1964)
The Killers (1946): 3.5;
The Killers (1964): 2.5
Disc: 4.0
[The Criterion Collection]

This may very well be the film noir release of 2003, a double set (actually a triple set) featuring two fully restored versions of Ernest Hemingway's *The Killers*, one made by Universal and directed by underappreciated Robert Siodmak, and the second a loose remake directed by Don Siegel (in bright color, no less) almost 20 years later. A 19-minute student film version, directed in 1956 in Russia by Andrei Tarkovsky, subtitled, is also included.

The original version of *The Killers* is a superb hard-boiled noir, featuring all the required noir icons, rendered especially attractive with this fine-grain, densely textured print that captures all the shades of black. Burt Lancaster's Ole "The Swede" Andersen, resigned to accept his imminent death at the hands of hired hit-men, admitting to a co-worker friend (who races through back alleyways, jumping over fences, in order to beat the killers to Swede's apartment, to try to save a friend's life) that he did a bad thing, is the heart and soul of noir, and of Hemingway. That is, a man accepts his fate without whining, without running, without fear. And when the hit men enter and star firing (William Conrad portrays one of the two thugs), Lancaster's hand grips the bedpost, resulting in a powerful moment.

Then following noir conventions, the story is told, and the mystery discovered, as insurance agent Edmund O'Brien, working with Swede's former boyhood friend, now a cop, track down all the pieces of the convoluted puzzle, all told in flashback snippets, and mostly snippets told out of order (which makes putting the puzzle together all the more interesting). Truly, this is a classic noir made in the editing room. Ava Gardner sizzles, as does Lancaster in his first classic performance, hulking and yet doe-faced. Just as life sneaks up on people when they aren't looking, the Swede is doomed the second the Albert Dekker character innocently ventures into the gas station where Swede works and eyeballs the now pathetic attendant. All the supporting performances are strong, and the film's cinematography is among the best-photographed noirs ever, masterfully shot by Elwood Bredell.

The Killers is best appreciated upon multiple viewings, allowing all the disjointed pieces to be assembled and understood.

Don Siegel, whom producer Mark Hellinger wanted to direct the 1946 original version, finally had the opportunity to direct the made-for-TV remake in 1964 (but released theatrically when it was deemed too violent for the small screen). The basic plot is radically changed with only the central theme remaining... why would a man allow himself to be gunned down in cold blood instead of trying to escape or fight for his life? Gunman Lee Marvin, working with young assistant Clu Gulager, is haunted by that question. After gunning down the former speed racing star John Cassavetes, who simply takes the fatal blows, Marvin cannot get his victim's solemn acceptance of his fate out of his mind, so he needs to unearth the man's past to put the pieces together. Along the way he encounters Ronald Reagan (looking presidential yet portraying the film's heavy) in his last film role before entering politics, as a slick gangster disguised as a corporate

businessman who is sugar-daddy to young and sexy Angie Dickinson, who happens to fall for Cassavetes, or does she? Is it love, or is she simply setting up the racer for the big fall? Lee Marvin, in his typical greasy criminal performance... always interestingly performed, learns the true secret before killing both Reagan, who dies like a man, and the cringing Dickinson, but he himself is shot and dies dramatically on the front lawn outside as the police speed down the street, Marvin holding his hand like a gun, just as children pretend; as he drops dead, his briefcase opens and spills the money. This brightly lit version of *The Killers* is not noir in execution, only in theme, with John Cassavetes accepting his fate, realizing there is no way out.

This Criterion Collection DVD two-disc set is loaded: a wonderful onscreen interview with writer/critic Stuart Kaminsky is included, trailers, radio dramatizations of the 1946 version (with Burt Lancaster and Shelley Winters), actor Stacy Keach reads the Hemingway short story aloud, Paul Schrader's pivotal article on film noir is reprinted, excerpts from Don Siegel's autobiography are presented, star Clu Gulager reflects, production drawings, stills and advertising are included, etc. For the price, everything has been included in the package, and when you consider both prints have never looked better, the value of this package goes even higher. For film noir fans, this is a must-have collection.

The Big Heat
Movie: 3.0; Disc: 3.0
[Columbia Pictures]

Film noir became sleazier and even more violent during the 1950s, and Fritz Lang's classic noir of 1953, *The Big Heat*, stands toe-to-toe with the best. Produced by Columbia, *The Big Heat* has a low-budget look and feel, but this only enhances the working class/no class criminal milieu that infests the screen. Glenn Ford plays the honest police detective, swimming with too many sharks, who is assigned the case of a department superior who committed suicide, amid hints that he was on the take. Ford, of course, gets too close to the answers, and the police hierarchy make it clear they don't want him to discover the truth, because too many not-so-innocent policemen would get caught in the so-called big heat. In early sequences, Ford is shown at home with his adoring wife, played by Jocelyn Brando, who savors their every moment together knowing his seemingly 24-hour work schedule could take him unexpectedly away from home at any moment. After we are drawn into their idyllic working-class life, she is murdered, blown apart in a car bomb meant for Ford. Thus, the kind and decent cop quits the force and, working from outside the system, vows to solve the case, no matter who gets exposed or hurt. Juxtaposed to the cop's relationship with his wife, we have a similar relationship existing in the underbelly of society, with Lee Marvin's sadistic hood character Vince Stone and his relationship to his kept girl Debby, played by Gloria Grahame, who enjoys her life of wealth (12-hour shopping sprees) and glamour that Stone provides. Debby's undoing is her moral conscience and physical attraction to the Glenn Ford character, causing her to help him and thus arouse suspicion in Stone (who is as protective of her as Ford was of his wife). Lee Marvin's Vince Stone is the archetype violent criminal trash, and Marvin has never been better in a role around which he built a career.

As was initiated with *Kiss Me Deadly*, film noir became exceptionally violent in the 1950s, and *The Big Heat* has one sequence of such utter violence that it could almost be classified as a horror movie (say, *The Hypnotic Eye*). Vince Stone, jealous that Gloria Grahame has been spending time with the ex-cop, punishes the overdone blonde by throwing scalding coffee into her face, scarring her for the rest of the movie (and she realizes that it is her looks that matter and are the only reason she is the mobster's moll), causing her to wear a gauze bandage across half of her face (until she pulls it back and reveals, shockingly, her deformity at the film's end).

Fritz Lang has directed many film noirs (*Clash by Night, Ministry of Fear, Fury, Scarlet Street* and *While the City Sleeps*) and *The Big Heat* is among his best; it might be considered his last classic movie. Glenn Ford's character is powerful, a good decent man operating in a corrupt world, but a man able to maintain his moral center and purpose even though his methods for good operate outside the system. But then we have the moral ambiguity created by Gloria Grahame's Debby, a mobster's mistress, yet a woman who ultimately jeopardizes her baby-doll world by taking a chance and doing the right thing, leaving her scarred and dead by film's end. But that's the universe of film noir, and Fritz Lang's exceptional police crime drama holds its audience spellbound.

Columbia's DVD print is exceptional with a few trailers and vintage advertising thrown in as the only extras.

Pennies from Heaven
Movie: 2.5; Disc: 3.0
[Columbia Pictures Home Video]

In 1936 the Depression was over, but Hollywood still produced movies that were primarily escapist film fare that helped Americans forget about the hard economic times that started to subside. Bing Crosby, the laidback crooner, stars in one of the best second-tier musicals of the period, playing a drifter who does not wish to accept any adult responsibility such as settling down, getting married, holding a job, etc. However, he does meet and grow attached to a young waif, played by the cute Edith Fallows, and in the best Shirley Temple tradition, he ends up getting romantically involved with his worst adversary, a social worker played by Madge Evans, and thus is able to adopt the child. But this is only after Crosby spends most of the movie running from authority figures and trying to convince himself that he does not wish to have anything to do with the young child who adores him. The audience knows better.

Interestingly enough, one of the plot's key points is the child's grandfather/guardian, Donald Meek (in one of his larger roles), joining forces with Crosby to open a haunted house-themed restaurant in the home Meek inherits from the child's late father. The ghostly accoutrements and mood is played largely for laughs and cheap shocks, but the house band, headed by youthful trumpet blower Louis Armstrong, plays the stereotyped Manton Moreland-style hi-jinks to the hilt. The restaurant gets by on the seat of its tattered pants, and Armstrong hopes to help the cause by providing real live chickens for the chicken dinners the restaurant serves daily. However, Armstrong and the band panic in the best comedic sense when the police raid the restaurant, having found out that Armstrong and company are stealing the chickens from a nearby farm.

The movie always plays larger than life, and even when dark clouds overpower the story, such as when the orphanage takes Edith Fallows away from Crosby and her grandfather, we simply know that things will turn out for the best. Crosby gets to sing many songs throughout, including the title song, and the good-hearted sentiment and humor is dosed consistently so the film never slumps. Crisply directed by Norman Z. McLeod, *Pennies from Heaven* is akin to the best Shirley Temple musical: it's short, it's snazzy, it's funny, it's heart-warming and it features many interesting musical interludes. What better way to forget about one's troubles by escaping into an idyllic world where even free spirits (hobos) can become the hero and win the heart of the leading lady in the last reel.

The movie features a beautiful high density print, but bonus trailers are the only extra.

Peter Lorre, Jules Munshin and Joseph Buloff face an unforgiving Ninotchka (Cyd Charisse) in 1957's *Silk Stockings*.

Above: Charisse with choreographer Eugene Loring on the set of Silk Stockings.
Below: Charisse's "Got the Red Blues."

Silk Stockings
Movie: 3.5; Disc: 3.5
[Warner Bros.]

While it never receives enough credit, Rouben Mamoulian's MGM musical of 1957 *Silk Stockings* is perhaps the last great MGM musical released and it remains in my top five of all time. While the musical was losing credibility, mainly due to budget cuts imposed during the Dore Shary regime (forcing *Brigadoon* to be filmed on obvious backstage sets, not Ireland, and making the switch from the expensive Technicolor to Ansco for musicals such as *Kiss Me Kate),* changing times and changing musical tastes meant that rock 'n' roll was in and Broadway musicals were out, at least for the time being. And after 1957 the MGM musical was pretty much a thing of the past.

But *Silk Stockings* was the last blast of creativity, featuring musical numbers by Cole Porter (including "Ritz Roll and Rock," an attempt to be hip by featuring an actual rock number, danced to by the 57-year-old Fred Astaire, that best sums up the death knell for the grand classical musical in five minutes), grand CinemaScope photography (in MetroColor, with Technicolor intensity) and clever direction by Rouben Mamoulian. Fred Astaire used his own choreographer Hermes Pan, while Eugene Loring handled the non-Astaire choreography. The production numbers are simply fabulous.

But is it the story and casting which makes *Silk Stockings* such a delight. Updating *Ninotchka* for the new generation, the great dancer Cyd Charisse assumes the Garbo role and proves she can carry a musical as lead character, not only lead dancer, with those gorgeous legs of hers. Fred Astaire is too old at 57 to play the romantic lead, but his debonair persona and his smooth, graceful movements defy the calendar and make his performance work. The supporting performances are outstanding, especially the energetic Janis Paige as lead actress in a movie who desires to turn a historic drama into a commercialized musical. Peter Lorre is delightful as one of three Russians sent to Paris to check up on the production, making sure the classically composed Russian musical score is not compromised. Peter Lorre, who cannot dance and who has a quirky sense of rhythm, does mighty fine in the production numbers that require him to move in sync with the other performers, and when it comes time to dance, the others dance while Lorre hunches down between pieces of furniture, a knife between his teeth, and he kicks up a storm Russian style, giving the production his all. Besides delivering some of the tastiest snippets of dialogue, Lorre's character becomes a standout, showing a side of Lorre that he had never before shown. The script is both breezy and dramatic, and the performers all carry their own weight to produce a totally satisfying musical that still holds up today. Cyd Charisse's dancing dazzles in the exuberant "Got the Red Blues" number.

Extras include a remembrance documentary starring Cyd Charisse, two vintage musical shorts (one, a terrific mini-musical stars a young and very hook-nosed Bob Hope early on in his screen career) and theatrical trailer. The soundtrack has been remixed in Dolby 5.1 surround and the movie now sounds as thrilling as it looks. Warner Bros. deserves kudos for presenting *Silk Stockings* as it hasn't looked or sounded since its theatrical release.

Christ in Concrete
Movie: 3.0; Disc: 3.5
[All Day Entertainment]

Edward Dmytryk's long-lost English film, *Christ in Concrete*, released mostly to raves in Europe in 1949, was buried theatrically in the United States mainly because Dymtryk was an infamous member of the Hollywood Blacklist (even though he was the only one of the original Hollywood Ten to defect, testify and name names, thus appearing as the lone "sell out" once the other nine were cleared). Anyway, Dmytryk's *Christ in Concrete* is a powerful artistic statement brimming with courage of political conviction. The film flirts with film noir, but really isn't noir; the film is social commentary and is decidedly anti-Capitalism. In visual look and tone, it reminds me of the similar themed movies directed by Elia Kazan in the 1950s, films such as *On the Waterfront*, *Streetcar Named Desire* and *East of Eden*, boasting intense Method-derived performances by Marlon Brando and James Dean. The cinematography and set design is mood evoking, creating a Brooklyn tenement with el-train passing in the background as immigrants live out the American Dream in the 1920s. The film's opening is very noirish in spirit, with Sam Wanamaker as the tortured Italian being smothered by imposing skyscrapers framed with ominous rolling clouds photographed from above looking down, making the character seem insignificant. His zombie-like walk up the tenement steps, into his apartment, confronting his wounded and betrayed wife who demands he return to the other woman is film noir at its most powerful and visual. However, from here on, the film opts for realism and social commentary demonstrating how the American Capitalist dream can be a trap, a seductive lure of evil, forcing the innocent immigrant to sell his soul for the dollar. It starts out bad when Sam Wanamaker's character agrees to marry, sight unseen, a young beauty from Italy; her only demand is that Wanamaker

provide her a house of their own. Quickly arranging a deal to at first rent (for the three day honeymoon) and then buy, on time payments, a fixer-upper cottage, Wanamaker does good by his word. When Wanamaker ultimately comes up with a total of $500 (at first the number was $750), he can live in the house. Soon Wanamaker, who works construction only two to three weeks per month, is praying for snow so he can make extra money by shoveling walkways for businesses. The bottom falls through when a friend offers Wanamaker the job of construction foreman, but the job has been won through a low bid that sacrifices the crew's health for profit (Wanamaker works with his friends and relatives of many years, people who trust him). Tragedy strikes twice, and the film's final images are stark as Wanamaker dies tragically by falling off scaffolding and into a vat of cement, where he is unable to move and soon finds himself drowning in the symbol of his life's work. In the coda, his family is paid $4,000 as a pay-off fee, allowing the family to at long last purchase their dream house and achieve the American dream. But at what price?

This All Day DVD contains a pristine 35mm print, audio commentary, isolated musical score, photo gallery, talent bio, featurette, etc. Once again it is amazing how the medium of DVD has returned forgotten movies to a general populace, making long-lost films available once again for viewing. No greater gift exists for the movie fan, and All Day is to be commended once again. Bravo!

Geremio (Sam Wanamaker) drowns literally in his work in *Christ in Concrete* from All Day.

Secret Agent X-9 (1937)
Movie: 3.0; Disc: 3.5
[VCI Entertainment]

Serials carry us back to more innocent times, times when heroes would constantly beat up the same villain, hold him at gunpoint, and still not dare fire the fatal shot in fear that he, the hero, would be taking the law into his own hands. *Secret Agent X-9*, first produced by Universal in 1937, was radically remade by Universal in 1945. Here, the comic strip written by Charles Flanders, based upon characters created by Dashiell Hammett, is a straight ahead Federal Agent detective yarn, one interestingly directed by the team of Ford Beebe and Clifford Smith. Playing against type, villain Blackstone is essayed by character actor Henry Brandon, who is most known for disguising himself under heavily made-up character roles (Barnaby in *Babes in Toyland*, Chief Scar in *The Searchers*, Fu Manchu in *Drums of Fu Manchu*, etc.). Here Brandon plays a dashing, handsome villain, one who works directly under the mysterious "chief" Brenda, international jewel thief. By the serial's conclusion the shocking mystery involving both Brenda and Blackstone is revealed and it still takes audiences by surprise.

Our hero X-9 is played by buoyant Scott Kolk, who does a workmanship job and whose right-hand man is David Oliver, who plays the sidekick role of the dedicated butler Pidge to perfection. Whether he delivers comic relief (a wonderful sequence in a tailor's shop has Pidge burning a hole in his own pants and taking an oversized replacement right off the shelf) or action-packed fisticuffs, Pidge is charming and one of the true stars of the production. Jean Rogers, Dale Arden from the Flash Gordon serials, portrays the mysterious Shara, heroine or accomplice to the villains, we never know for sure until the serial reaches past its halfway point. But Monte Blue, portraying the distinguished Baron who is trying to recover his nation's crown jewels, stolen by Brenda, appears to be playing a role tailor-made for Bela Lugosi (looking as Lugosi looked two years earlier in Universal's *The Invisible Ray*). While Blue is marvelous, Lugosi would have been superior.

The serial is filled with action, good fight sequences, effective cliffhanger endings and the pacing never lags. The set pieces are quite visual and hold the viewer's interest: a tourist pirate's ship, docked at the harbor, that shelters the gang of modern-day cutthroats; a country estate with fake fireplaces and underground tunnels leading to getaway speedboats below; a well-mounted harbor community of shops populated by rough and tumble watermen. For classic movie fans, besides the villainous turn by Henry Brandon, up-and-coming Lon Chaney, Jr. looks youthful and handsome as a member of Brenda's gang.

This VCI DVD features a fine-grain 35mm print with excellent contrast, in pristine shape with a strong soundtrack. Extras include bios for the cast and crew and a selection of serial trailers. *Secret Agent X-9* was produced for a Saturday afternoon matinee audience, but for this gracefully aging adult, the serial held my interest and kept me involved for all 12 chapters.

Secret Agent X-9 (1945)
Movie: 3.0; Disc: 3.5
[VCI Entertainment]

Eight years after the release of Universal's *Secret Agent X-9*, Universal went to the well one more time for a drastically re-sculpted remake. Instead of recasting the serial (now 13 chapters long) as just another detective thriller, the new *Secret Agent X-9* becomes a World War II spy thriller, occurring on Shadow Island, a neutral Asian island where criminal Japanese, Germans, Australians and Americans can commingle unmolested. The major action on Shadow Island occurs in the island saloon, which resembles a redecorated saloon set from *Destry Rides Again* and is presided over by self-confessed dictator and ruler of the island, Lucky (Cy Kendall), a benevolent despot as long as Japan does not reclaim the island for itself. In this chapterplay world everyone might very well be a self-serving villain, especially the red herring Checkers-playing recluse Solo, played by Universal contract player Samuel S. Hinds, who never seems to move from his regular perch in the saloon. But Occidental actress Victoria Horne portrays chief villain Nabura, the wily Asian spy who is out to destroy X-9 by all dastardly means possible. Creating an Asian-stereotyped villain, Nabura speaks in deliberate, clipped English, usually punctuating her sentences with insidious smiles and one-liners. She seldom looks anyone in the eye when speaking to them and her arrogance and air of superiority makes her villainy memorable.

But on the hero's side we have a youthful Lloyd Bridges portraying our title character, helped by superior second banana Keye Luke who portrays a Chinese agent Ah Fong. Keye Luke is usually associated with playing Number One Son in Charlie Chan mysteries, and in these performances his comic timing, inexperience and resulting stupidity (requiring father Chan to bail him out) shines through, molding his Charlie Chan performances into little more than comic relief. However, in *Secret Agent X-9* Keye Luke portrays a suave agent, very clever and also a good physical fighter who can make a leap or exercise a kick with aplomb. Shamefully, Keye Luke was not utilized more frequently in such heroic performances and is best remembered for playing Asian lunkheads. Jan Wiley, portraying an Australian agent seemingly working for the Axis Powers, is competent as the spunky heroine.

Secret Agent X-9 ultimately aces the original serial by nature of Bridges' superior heroic performance and with all the impressive set pieces used to convey the action. We have Japanese fliers in airplanes dive-bomb the coast of the island, trying to riddle X-9 full of holes; we have submarines torpedoing ships; we have Japanese troops taking over the island and blowing up buildings; we have secret meetings, hidden rooms and plastic surgery; we have full-blown bar fights sometimes resulting in death; etc. And all this occurs so the Japanese can steal a secret formula from an American professor so that a synthetic airplane fuel can be created and thus aid the Japanese in winning the war. The action is non-stop and the plot credible enough to maintain interest. Every person on the island is seemingly a spy, working for some foreign government, and even the people we first suspect of un-American leanings may suddenly turn out to be agents working for the good guys. The directing team of Lewis D. Collins and Ray Taylor keeps all the shenanigans moving along with a sense of fun.

Max Allan Collins, pulp fiction writer and author of the graphic novel *The Road to Perdition*, supplies audio commentary and conducts a telephone conversation with Beau Bridges, who talks about father Lloyd. Other extras include a photo gallery, bio and filmography of the cast and crew and selected trailers for other serials released through VCI. The print used is pristine, making *Secret Agent X-9* a revelation and one of the finer serials ever made.

Drums of Fu Manchu
Movie: 3.5; Disc: 3.0
[VCI Entertainment]

When it comes to naming classic serials, titles such as *Fighting Devil Dogs, Flash Gordon* and *Zorro's Fighting Legion* jump out. But Republic's classic serial, *Drums of Fu Manchu*, remains one of the best, especially when considering Henry Brandon's star-turn portraying sinister evil, Dr. Fu Manchu. In fact many consider Brandon's performance as Fu Manchu to be perhaps the best performance in any serial (a genre not typically remembered for Academy Award–winning caliber performances).

What makes *Drums of Fu Manchu* classic is the simple audacity apparent in every aspect of the production. Directed by the team of William Witney and Joseph English (the most renowned serial directing team ever) and occupying 15 chapters and running 269 minutes, *Drums of Fu Manchu* never drags and the action shifts so dramatically (from the American West Coast to isolated forts under attack by renegade Asian tribes in China and India) that the story never appears redundant. We have Fu Manchu's Dacoits (zombies under the direct will of Fu Manchu, who operated on their brains, leaving large crisscrossing scars on their foreheads) attacking a country estate by walking on electrical wiring leading to the house. The wily Dacoits always attack unexpectedly, able to sneak into every building much like cockroaches. And as is true of every Republic serial, the fistfights are spectacular with stunt players leaping into mid-air, flipping over backwards, running and falling and taking their share of punches with knives thrusting all over the screen. Fu Manchu, always polite yet sinister in the way he simply looks at his captives, dominates the screen with

every gesture and the sheer force of his presence. Unfortunately, Gloria Franklin, who plays Fu's daughter, is merely adequate, vastly inferior to the similar sexually charged performance by Myrna Loy in 1932's *The Mask of Fu Manchu*, which starred Boris Karloff as the Asian dictator.

Henry Brandon as Fu Manchu in *Drums of Fu Manchu*, 1943

Drums of Fu Manchu is almost always played for horror in the first half (with action and adventure dominating the second half) occurring at West Coast settings, with Fu's henchman seemingly impervious to doors, walls, ceilings and locks. Some great tension is mounted when a historic wax museum, housed by living Dacoits, becomes a trap for unsuspecting Sir Nayland Smith and his party (and having Dwight Frye portray the curator was a nice touch). Later, Fu and his forces attack the country estate of an eccentric during a moody rainstorm, with lightning illuminating the monstrous approach of the Asian demon from the woodsy terrain surrounding the house. Very spooky stuff that is well photographed and edited.

One problem constantly perturbs me about this serial. Fu Manchu is dastardly, even pushing the button that allows our hero Allen Parker (Robert Kellard) to fall through a trap door into water occupied by a monstrous squid ready for feeding. Even after surviving that ordeal, Parker confronts Fu or his Dacoits by holding them at bay with a pistol, never once thinking of blasting the Asian devil to the land of his ancestors. After having the upper hand and losing it every time to treachery and mayhem, none of the heroes ever considers simply filling Fu with several rounds of lead. It's very frustrating!

By movie's end Fu Manchu's car dives over a cliff, but the lucky warrior only sports a sling around his shoulder as a sign of any physical damage, swearing to his gods to yet conquer the world. Obviously a sequel was in the offing, but sadly, one never materialized. *Drums of Fu Manchu* has the acting (with the exception of deadly dull William Royle as Nayland Smith), the direction, the cinematography, the story and the action sequences to concoct a superior, classic serial. Unfortunately, while VCI offers the best-looking 35mm print ever made available on home video, the original source material, the original negatives, must be missing because every print of this serial looks second or third generation and has a decidedly washed-out look. The VCI DVD release offers a full-color booklet written by historian Eric Hoffman. Audio commentary is executed by Richard Valley and the extra features include a photo gallery, trailers and bios and filmography of the major cast and crew members. Perhaps one day original negatives will be found, but for now, this VCI presentation is the best we will ever hope to get. For anyone who loves serials, this may very well be the best.

Radar Men from the Moon
Movie: 2.5; Disc: 3.0
[Hal Roach/ Image Entertainment]

By 1951 Republic, king of the serial-makers, was well past its prime. In fact many people consider *King of the Rocket Men*, the first in the Rocket Man trilogy, to be Republic Picture's last great serial.

Radar Men from the Moon, introducing the character of Commando Cody, Rocket Man (played by the almost-milquetoast George Wallace), is a fantastical serial that plays very loose with science, even for 1951. For instance, constantly throughout the serial, Commando Cody and his crew fly a rocketship (which looks like a bullet with fins) to the moon and back... without the Earthly atmosphere changing color (no black vastness, no stars, no meteorites). The flight seems more like an airplane flight from the East to the West Coast, not a jaunt in outer space! And of course the moon civilization, looking like Greek- or Roman-derived megastructures, is headed by nasty serial perennial Roy Barcroft. It seems the Moon people have discovered an alternative to Uranium to produce atomic weaponry (in laser canons, in ray guns, in volcanic-erupting atomic bombs) to conquer the Earth, because the Moon's atmosphere is too thin and food cannot any longer be grown there.

On Earth Clayton Moore, television's Lone Ranger, becomes one of two thugs who serve the Moon emissary to wreak havoc to soften up the Earthlings for invasion. We know we are in for a long ride when Commando Cody and his sidekick face Clayton Moore and his sidekick, and in at least three fistfight battles, Clayton Moore's posse kicks the asses of Commando and comrade. Psychologically, it is depressing that in every physical battle that Commando Cody gets his lights punched out, every time. Only when wearing his Rocket Man suit does he seem to have the edge to prevail.

Far too many cliffhangers involve cars speeding off the road and going over embankments exploding into a fiery blaze below. Seldom does the viewer get the feeling that our heroes are ever in danger and we simply know too readily that somehow Commando Cody will not die. The outrageous shenanigans involving Moon cars, death rays from the back of trucks, mountains melting into raging seas of lava, rocketships evading horrible death rays and poison gas being pumped into Commando's headquarters provide a fun romp that while straining credibility does entertain. The serial is mercifully short, running a brief 169 minutes in 12 chapters. The print used is a tad soft but pristine with fine-grain contrast and without a splice or scratch to be found. Image really came up with superb source material here. Extras include serial trailers and that's about it. The entire serial is put on one disc and is well worth the money.

Mandrake, the Magician
Movie: 3.0; Disc: 3.5
[VCI Entertainment]

Columbia was the bargain-basement studio in the serial market, but entries such as *Mandrake, the Magician* prove that even non-Republic entries can be entertaining and suspenseful. Warren Hull, a marvelous serial hero, portrays the affluent Mandrake who lives in a gated mansion that somehow is not impervious to entry by the bad guys at any given hour of the day. By the serial's end we genuinely feel sorry for Mandrake's obedient butler who gets the tar beat out of him on several occasions and simply is picked up off the floor by rescuers and declares all he needs is to lay down a few minutes in his room.

Friend and assistant Dr. Houston (Forbes Murray) has concocted a radium machine, to be used by the scientific and medical community to do good, while evil masked villain The Wasp wants to use the contraption to disrupt the American communications system and thus conquer the world. Working out of his home, Dr. Houston's laboratory, even when locked, somehow can be accessed by the henchmen of The Wasp. For instance, in one sequence Houston is working while locked in his laboratory, preparing for a demonstration during a formal party at his home. A knock occurs on the door, and when Houston opens the door and is asked how things are coming, he states he'll be along in a few minutes. As soon as he locks the door on his left, evil henchmen enter the lab from the right, almost as if there were no wall to obstruct their admittance. Only such silliness can occur in the world of chapterplays.

Mandrake is quite dashing and Columbia keeps the action moving, even if the quality of the fistfights is not up to Republic standards. However, with right-hand man Lothar (Al Kikume), who shamelessly refers to Mandrake as Master, the magician is almost invincible. Almost magically, Lothar manages to appear on the scene whenever Mandrake needs assistance or whenever fancy driving is required to escape the villains or expertly manipulate the vehicle to avoid sudden death. Lothar is there to protect his master for another day.

Mandrake, the Magician is one of those serials where the fancifully costumed villain, who always appears projected onto a large screen to deliver instructions to his cronies, turns out to be a member of the circle of friends of Mandrake and it is the audience's job to guess which "friend" is actually The Wasp. Of course the serial plays with the concept of red herrings and several times a close friend says something that could be interpreted as being sinister or he quickly shifts his eyes, just to plant a suggestion that he might be the one. Unfortunately, the villain is perhaps too easily guessed at, but the revelation at the serial's end is still exciting. Produced in 1939, an important year for chapterplays, the directing team of Sam Nelson and Norman Deming does a wonderful job of creating suspense and action, all neatly framed around Warren Hull's dashing turn as the heroic magician. As usual, the VCI print is absolutely spectacular with nary a flaw. The print features intense contrast with a strong soundtrack. Extras include trailers, cast and crew bios and a poster gallery. *Mandrake, the Magician*, not one of the more well-known serial entries, is definitely worth the price of admission.

The Rogues Tavern
Movie: 2.5; Disc: 3.0
[Alpha Video]

Alpha Video is the Rodney Dangerfield of DVD home video, the little company that appears in every Sam's Club, every Border's, every Best Buy store from East to West Coast. Alpha Video titles typically sell for six dollars and feature beautifully designed covers. Unfortunately, unlike Image or Anchor Bay, Alpha Video DVDs are mastered mostly from 16mm prints and do not have the pristine look of higher-cost DVD releases. But darn it, where else can one see *The Rogues Tavern* and many other releases of Alpha Video? And remember, customers do not pay $20 or more, they only pay $6.

And to be quite honest, seeing this perfectly acceptable 16mm print of *The Rogues Tavern*, complete with slightly scratchy soundtrack, a few jump-cut splices and a wavering frame here and there, is akin to watching a 16mm print in the basement of George Stover, a ritual repeated by movie fans across the U.S.A.

The Rogues Tavern, released by Puritan Pictures in 1936, is a worthy member of the Old Dark House murder-mystery subgenre. Directed by Robert F. Hill, the film stars Wallace Ford in one of his wisecracking leads, along with Joan Woodbury, Jack Mulhall and Barbara Pepper. The movie concerns Wallace Ford, a detective, and his desire to marry beautiful blonde Joan Woodbury. They arrange to have a Justice of the Peace meet them at the Red Rock Tavern, and while arriving by bus at the tavern, every single resident appears to be either a sinister predator (an elderly woman reads the cards of a tenant and predicts his death, with glaring, beady eyes saying it all) or a victim waiting to be dispatched. Minutes after arriving at the tavern, a horrendous scream upstairs attracts all the assembled who spot a large dog running off as the predicted victim lies dying ("the room is growing dark; I can't breathe"), his throat apparently slashed by canine teeth. Soon other victims are claimed, in exactly the same way, as the second victim goes outside with a gun to try to finish off the dog (tell me, what other movie features a pet dog as chief red herring of grisly murders).

It soon becomes apparent that the human killer uses phony canine teeth to tear out the victim's throats, and quick-witted Wally Ford discovers that all the assembled people, from across the country, have been specifically called to come to the Red Rock Tavern at this time. It is revealed that all of them are involved in smuggling and selling expensive stolen gems (all except Ford and his fiancée). Soon the original owner of the tavern, a long lanky figure with thick lenses that magnify the size of his eyes, is seen prowling around outside and in the dank cellar. Mysterious, threatening recordings are amplified throughout the lobby, as more victims are claimed. By the movie's end, the maniacal murderer is revealed, a person, of course, never to be suspected, although late in the movie a series of darting, intense eye movements in close-up is designed to make the audience suspect that this person is hiding a dark secret.

For a creaky and atmospheric whodunit, *The Rogues Tavern* is very entertaining. Lacking a musical score that would definitely benefit the production, the cinematography by William Hyer is first-rate and the performances stereotyped yet sinister, with everyone considered a prime suspect. The movie runs a brisk 70 minutes and the direction keeps everyone guessing and in suspense for the total running time. It is nice to see for the first time a movie never seen before, and it is even nicer to find *The Rogues Tavern* so entertaining and well done to boot.

Destry Rides Again
Movie: 3.0; Disc: 3.5
[Universal DVD]

Destry Rides Again is another in a long list of wonderful movies produced in 1939, a Western that isn't quite a Western, starring James Stewart and Marlene Dietrich, with dastardly Brian Donlevy along for the ride. Wonderful support comes from Mischa Auer (creating a wonderful characterization of a Russian trying to become a cowboy) and Charles Winninger (transcending the typical town drunk role to create something quite profound and moving).

The movie is not really a spoof or send-up, for the tone is ultimately heartfelt and the movie takes itself seriously. However, with Marlene Dietrich portraying the town saloon girl who is the entertainer as well, the movie becomes quite quirky with Dietrich performing in rhinestone outfits wearing her cowboy hat and singing and dancing to songs such as "The Boys in the Back Room." James Stewart plays a role that is a precursor to his similar performance 20 years later in *The Man Who Shot Liberty Valance*. Both heroes fight most effectively with words and are thus considered sissy-cowboys by the town's community. Destry is in fact a master of the six-shooter and has opportunity to demonstrate his prowess; however, his father was a marshal who was murdered in cold blood, shot in the back, so Destry abhors the use of weapons and plans to clean up the town without resorting to violence. Gentleman villain and titular town leader Brian Donlevy, who at first fears the onset of new law (after he has the former sheriff gunned down in cold blood), soon appoints the town drunk as sheriff and milquetoast Destry as deputy, thinking they will play right into his hands. Of course he is wrong.

Jimmy Stewart and Marlene Dietrich in *Destry Rides Again*

Directed by George Marshall, *Destry Rides Again* transcends the genre because of its ever-changing tone. The film is playful when Destry first arrives by stagecoach and is seen by the community carrying a parasol; the film's tone is lighthearted in a barroom brawl scene when Frenchie (the Germanic Dietrich) literally tears the bar apart in a comical fight involving Destry; the film is heart-wrenching when the new sheriff is shot in the back and dies after delivering a poignant speech to Destry, who comforts the dying sheriff in a sensitive manner; the film is hard-hitting when Destry finally puts on his father's guns and heads out to bring Brian Donlevy and gang to justice. At times the film does not seem able to settle into what it wishes to be: a drama or a comedy, but ultimately, it seems to be a drama with comic overtones. Whatever it is, it is simply wonderful.

The print used by Universal is pristine with deep density and a strong soundtrack. Whether you enjoy the musical numbers with Marlene Dietrich (whose

Mad About Movies 4   65

performance is very effective), the comedy, the dramatic gunplay, the confrontation between good and bad guys or simply the marvelous character interaction, *Destry Rides Again* seems to please everyone and also features a marvelous James Stewart performance.

What a Girl Wants
Movie: 2.5; Disc: 3.5
[Warner Home Video]

As the back cover boasts, *What a Girl Wants* continues the genre started by Disney's *The Parent Trap* where adolescent girls must establish their own identity outside the world of their parents (and bring separated parents together once again). Frisky Amanda Bynes is simply cute and becomes a perfect role model for "girl power" adolescent girls. She is pretty but not too beautiful, innocently sexy but also clumsy, good-humored and quite normal. She has resided for 17 years with her nomad musician mother (Kelly Preston) and lives in a Chinatown apartment. It seems mother loved British aristocrat Colin Firth and was ready to marry, when his family and advisers made it clear that her presence would endanger his social status, so she left him to save his career, never telling him she was pregnant (since Firth was and is the love of her life).

Of course mother plans to spend the rest of her life alone, playing her music, raising her wonderful daughter. Until one day Daphne (Bynes) announces she plans to fly to England and present herself to Firth as his daughter, to try to bond and create some sort of relationship with the stuck-up Brit who is now running for political office. The movie develops in the generally accepted pattern that at first her presence is awkward but soon father Firth seems to recapture the wildness of his youth (putting on the old leather rock 'n' roll pants and playing air guitar, assuming dramatic rock poses, in front of the mirror) which becomes upsetting to his political adviser (Jonathan Pryce). Daphne tends to undo the stuffiness of coming-out parties and helps unpopular debutantes find themselves and happiness. In the meanwhile Bynes falls in love with a musician who happens to perform at all the society benefits, but to please her father, she tends to reject who she really is and tries to become the proper British daughter that her father needs her to be to win the election. But by movie's end, both father and daughter learn Shakespeare's greatest lesson—to thine own self be true—and he forfeits the election and Daphne reverts to her formerly funky true self.

Of course all ends well, with mother and father united in America and Daphne being accepted to college in England so she can spend time with her Brit boyfriend. Formula, formula, formula, but the performances and fresh plot twists make this the perfect movie for young girls ready to blossom into womanhood. For adults, the movie is comic and romantic and entertain-

What most big girls want is Colin Firth (*What a Girl Want*s).

ing fluff, better than most movies of this ilk and contains several references to the BBC *Pride and Prejudice*, where Firth portrayed Mr. Darcy. Extras include multiple audio commentaries, several documentaries, trailers, etc. The print used is vibrant with good Dolby 5.1 surround. *What a Girl Wants* is diverting entertainment and Amanda Bynes emerges as a talent to watch.

Narc
Movie: 3.5; Disc: 3.5
[Paramount Home Video]

Cop dramas used to be hard-hitting and cutting edge (remember *Dog Day Afternoon*, remember *Serpico*, remember *Dirty Harry*), but of late, the subgenre has grown flaccid. However the low-budget Joe Carnahan movie, *Narc*, returns the cop drama to that desperate edge of cinematic artistry. Carnahan favors a slightly busy style, at one point dividing his screen into four segments showing four different points of view of the same basic action. Clever yes, but almost too showy for its own good. Generally Carnahan allows character to unveil his crisscross plot of intrigue, deception and ultimately police corruption. The little things here matter, such as showing us the dark and dingy homes that these cops return to, decorated with furniture that was passé 20 years ago. By the end of the movie, why anyone would want to become a policeman seems insane to me. As depicted in this movie, cops become too aligned with the very dregs of society they are supposed to be putting away. The morality of the police becomes one pubic hair removed from the amorality of the criminals and the movie blurs the lines between good guy and bad guy. Yes, this theme has been illustrated before, but in this gritty and hard-hitting production, the theme is reinvented for a new generation who want to keep it real.

Thus, the plot is not new, but the stylistic means of delivering it is innovative and fresh. But what makes this film great is its riveting performances by Jason Patric and Ray Liotta (all beefed up for this performance). Patric portrays a formerly suspended officer, Tellis, who became addicted while posing undercover. But now he is back

on track but still in trouble. At the film's beginning he is chasing down a criminal on the run, and forced to shoot to bring him down, but a stray bullet hits a pregnant woman causing her to lose her baby. Appearing before a review board, Tellis demonstrates he kowtows to no one and abruptly walks out of the hearing when he's heard enough. Still reinstated, he is told he can have the desk job he desires (out in the field is simply too much for this fallen warrior) if he brings in a conviction for another undercover cop who was seemingly murdered in a drug deal gone bad. Furthermore, Tellis is assigned to work with the slain officer's former partner, Oak (Ray Liotta), a loose canon who tells Tellis point blank that he will break every rule necessary to bring in his partner's murderer. In the best dramatic sense, plot evolves from such character and each actor creates a fractured, multi-dimensioned and realistic performance. As would be expected, neither person is likable and by the film's end, when one of the cops turns out to be corrupt, it is difficult to distinguish between the cop we like and the cop we hate. In fact it is Busta Rhymes' performance that resonates, as one of the supposed cop killers. He and his friend are being set up for the crime where neither one of them is guilty of murder (of dealing drugs, yes, but murder, *no*) and both are ritualistically tortured and forced to confess into a tape recorder.

Bottom line, *Narc* is not pretty and is not uplifting. It is a fictional journey into the corrupted world of law enforcement where the cops are not really any better than the criminals they oppose, yet it rings true. The movie is riveting in a vile way, almost to the extent that the audience wishes to shower after watching the movie and get the grit and filth out of its pores. However, it is exceptionally crafted cinema and extremely well acted. While Ray Liotta is wonderful, Jason Patric is even better and his heroic actions at the conclusion are suddenly turned around to reveal him to be just as tainted as anyone else. Extras include audio commentaries, trailers, documentaries, etc. Simply put, *Narc* returns the cop drama to the artistry exhibited a generation ago... it is almost too honest and brutal for its own good.

Shanghai Knights
Movie: 3.5; Disc: 3.5
[Touchstone DVD]

Who said movie comedy teams are dead?!! Jackie Chan and Owen Wilson are this generation's Laurel and Hardy, Blues Brothers, Hope and Crosby. They are that good. But different! It's more like Gene Kelly and Donald O'Connor. First of all we have Jackie Chan whose kung-fu antics, always wonderful even though Chan is no longer the spring chicken he used to be, are revealed to be closer to dance choreography than kung fu. In fact, during one fight Chan dons an umbrella and does a marvelous homage to the tune "Singin' in the Rain," rendered as a tribute to Gene Kelly. Chan may have gained notoriety for his martial arts skills, but in this film his dancing talents become front and center (perhaps, at advancing years, he realizes he cannot kung-fu fight forever, but as a dancer his career can continue). Even his opening tribute to the Keystone Cops is choreographed to be more musical than karate.

And Owen Wilson is the shifty verbal comedian, the one who loses the entire fortune from the first movie (*Shanghai Noon*) and is reduced to working as a gigolo/waiter in an exclusive hotel. He becomes the Bob Hope of his generation, the smooth-talking Oliver Hardy, the crafty Groucho Marx. During one burning building sequence, Jackie Chan wants to catapult Wilson to safety by thrusting him skyward. Wilson, in brilliant form, utters, no way, implying that he is no physical stuntman, that he uses his brain, not his brawn. Thus their characters and personality are solidified.

Besides the artistry in Jackie Chan's choreographed violence and fighting, the movie's plot, involving Victorian London with Sir Arthur Conan Doyle and Jack the Ripper, is straight from the pulp magazines, but the intertwining of literary characters and celebrities (including Charlie Chaplin) is cleverly conceived. Just like the Bob Hope Road pictures, the plot keeps moving deliciously forward, jumping between serious action (the slaughter of Jackie Chan's father and the capture of his sister) and comic hi-jinks (in the sequence in the hotel when Jackie Chan is told by Owen Wilson to charge a woman for sexually servicing her, Wilson intrudes into Chan's room to find the terrified Chan contorting his body to stretch the woman's back in the best sense of comic perfection), ultimately resulting in a movie that is best described as action-adventure, comedy and spoof. For once we like the comic heroes and we care for the things they care about (family honor, measuring up to a father's image of what we should be, being the protective older brother, playing fair with one another, etc.). The action is non-stop, the laughs non-stop and the artistic cleverness creates a film that is one of my favorites of the past year. Extras include audio commentaries, deleted scenes, fight bloopers (standard in any Jackie Chan production), documentaries and a wonderful print with full-bodied sound. *Shanghai Knights*, for me, is even better than the original entry, but both are wonderful movies for the entire family. Welcome Owen Wilson and Jackie Chan, the Laurel and Hardy of a new generation!

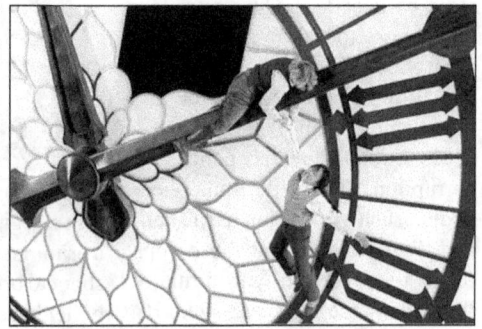

Jackie Chan and Owen Wilson make an appealing odd couple in *Shanghai Knights*.

Up in the Air
Movie 2.0; Disc: 3.0
[Alpha Video]

The comedy teaming of Frankie Darro and Mantan Moreland is hampered by one thing—Frankie Darro, whose pint-size arrogance, which seems clever at first, soon grates as his dominance of the movie only makes the viewer wish for more Mantan. Darro is at his best at the movie's beginning, trying to impress the cute young female receptionist (Marjorie Reynolds) at the radio station by telling her she can have a singing audition (her actual goal) and that this other girl will gladly cover for her. However, the glad-handing Darro is soon revealed to be a subordinate at the station, and he doesn't really have any artistic clout other than listening to Reynolds sing and realizing that she is talented.

Soon, in a closed studio during a radio broadcast, star singer Lorna Gray is murdered, shot through the heart, and everyone assembled becomes a red herring having a motive for murder. Frankie Darro and custodian Mantan Moreland become amateur sleuths attempting to solve the case. Whenever the multi-talented Moreland is on screen, the film rumbles with tension and a solid comedic vibe. Whether Mantan is acting afraid or performing a soft shoe dance, the man is mesmerizing. But far too often the plot focuses on Darro's romantic subplot or the plot machinations that take away from Moreland's delightful interludes.

The mystery plot is quite conventional and the actual murderer is someone that tends to drift off the movie's radar and becomes almost forgotten. However, for a 62-minute B picture released in 1940, the antics are diverting enough and again only point out how underused a comic talent Mantan Moreland was. Fortunately, this Alpha Video DVD features a worn but quite satisfactory 16mm print with good sound, and the movie is thankfully unedited (considering its historic frame of reference and the political correctness police who last banned a summer cable TV festival of Charlie Chan movies).

Once again, very few movie fans have ever seen the several movies comprising the teaming of Darro and Moreland, and while one movie does not justify the current contention that Moreland was in the running to be one of the Three Stooges, it is quite clear that Moreland's comic style and timing would have lent itself beautifully to the Stooges' style. Now is the time for a resurgence of the cinema of Mantan Moreland! And we thank Alpha Video for presenting this seldom-seen comedy mystery.

The Sphinx
Movie 3.0: Disc: 3.0
[Alpha Video]

In 1933 Lionel Atwill had two massive horror/mystery hits with *The Mystery of the Wax Museum* and *The Vampire Bat*, after scoring a homerun with his red herring role in 1932's *Doctor X*, establishing Atwill as a premier Hollywood villain. In this 1933 Monogram production, Atwill plays both the red herring and the villain, impossible as this may seem.

The movie starts out as a dapper Atwill, portraying Jerome Breen, stockbroker, impeccably dressed, walks right up to the Italian maintenance worker in a closed office building, and with his distinct authoritative voice, asks what time it is. The Italian asks him a slew of questions, but with a polite smile, the Atwill character ignores them all and slowly walks off. Inside the office is the strangled corpse of a dead man, with Atwill obviously the murderer.

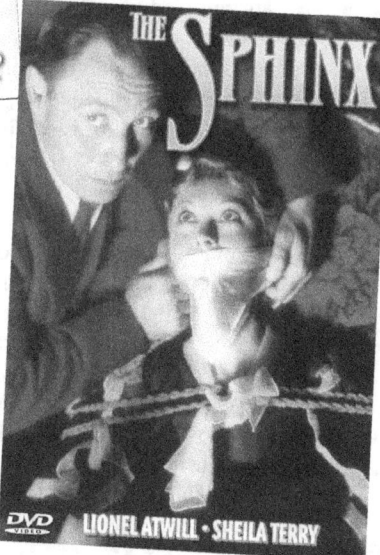

Once Breen is arrested and stands trial, it is medically proven that Breen is a deaf mute and is unable to utter even a sound, let alone speak. However, the Italian heard the philanthropist speak and thus Breen is cleared of the murder charge. Atwill's performance in court is very interesting, very low-key, with sympathetic eyes. He signs his responses to the court-appointed translator and seems very secure and in control. Audiences see none of the wild-eyed hysterics that we commonly associate with Atwill.

Soon other victims, all involved in the stockbroker business, are mysteriously found murdered in identically the same manner. A reporter and police inspector Riley (Robert Ellis) are on the case, and Breen fails to respond to even the firing of a police pistol, holding on to his deaf mute ruse. However, when the inspector starts banging on the piano keys, Breen's eyes perk right up and the usual Atwill wild-eyed reaction makes a return appearance. Strangely, that very night, the inspector is murdered, strangled in his bed. As it turns out, the far right key on the piano, a silent note, opens a hidden wall revealing a secret room housing Breen's identical twin brother, the deal mute who stood trial. He creates an iron-clad alibi for Breen, who goes out of his way to speak to someone after the murder is committed. In a hysterical sequence, as the new police inspector is playing the piano, no one looks at Atwill, but the camera constantly cuts to intense close-ups where Atwill is on the verge of blowing a blood vessel, hoping against hope that the cop does not hit the hidden wall key. Here, the movie goes way, way over the top, but Atwill's performance is crazed, as a contrast to his humble, quiet and low-key performance in the rest of the movie.

The Sphinx is a solid B programmer, featuring the type of witty urban jargon common to *Dr. X*, establishing the lead characters as hard-nosed if not quite hard-boiled. Atwill, while his performance at the end does go over the top, overall submits an intriguing characterization of twin brothers. The film comes recommended for Atwill's performance alone. It is little more than a routine B mystery, but with the plot surprises and interesting performances, *The Sphinx* rises above to become a superior early B entry. Alpha Video's 16mm print is fine and the few jarring jump cuts do not undermine the intrigue and suspense.

Lionel Atwill is up to his usual evil deeds as he plays twin brothers in *The Sphinx*.

Bulldog Drummond in Africa
Movie: 2.5; Disc: 3.0
[Alpha Video]

John Howard assumes the key role of Drummond in this short 58-minute entry in the *Bulldog Drummond* series, one that opens with perhaps the most bizarre beginning in any entry in the series. Drummond, along with his manservant (E.E. Clive, the Burgomaster from *Bride of Frankenstein*), are talking in Drummond's study when it is revealed that neither man is wearing pants. It seems today is Drummond's wedding day, and to prevent anything from interfering with the nuptials, friends have taken the pants of the two males and are requiring them to stay put at home. The snappy dialogue between Clive and Howard keeps the movie perky and involving. Unluckily, Bulldog's fiancée Phyllis (Heather Angel) goes to see wedding guest Colonel Neilson of Scotland Yard and finds the house inhabited by a suspicious looking J. Carrol Naish, who claims he now lives in the residence. Sneaking around the corner outside, hiding in the shrubbery, Phyllis witnesses the abduction of Neilsen, who is carried unconscious to his own car by Naish and accomplices.

Before Phyllis can get word to Drummond, the abducted Scotland Yard inspector is flown to Morocco,

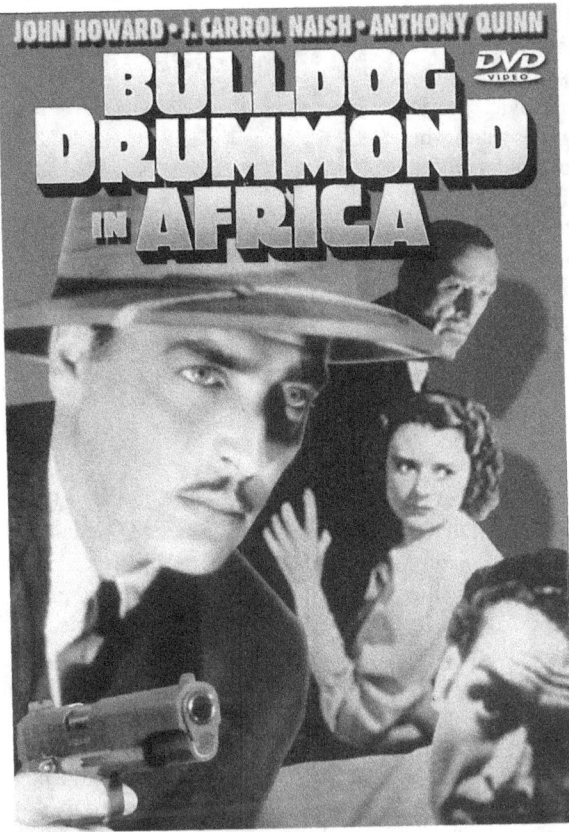

where J. Carrol Naish, as Richard Lane, heads a spy network. Of course, all the officials in Morroco know Lane by another name, and he is the most trusted citizen in the vicinity. So when Bulldog Drummond and friends arrive and point the accusing finger at Lane, everyone thinks that Drummond is the evil one. When Drummond is escorted to his plane and told to leave the country, little does he know that his plane has been tampered with and a bomb has been attached, set to explode one hour after the plane leaves. However, dumb luck forces the plane to land prematurely and the crew just manages to exit before the plane explodes in flames.

In Africa, Richard Lane uses a wild lion as his torture device to make people talk, in this case when Neilsen is tied to a tree and persuaded to speak. However, we know he's made of sterner stuff, for in an earlier scene, Neilsen maintains his British cool as the verbal barbs fly back and forth, with Neilsen delivering the most intelligent insult before smashing his toasting glass to the stone floor below, a smile on his lips.

Somehow the lack of budget makes the thrilling climax not as thrilling and action-packed as it might have been, had the budget been more substantial. But the hour-long B mystery adventure holds our interest, mainly because of the clever dialogue and interesting relationships that exist between the central characters. Once again the 16mm print used by Alpha Video is just fine and the movie becomes a pleasing entry in the Bulldog Drummond series.

Winchester '73
Movie: 3.5; Disc: 3.0
[Universal DVD]

In 1950 director Anthony Mann was ready to catapult Universal's Westerns from the kiddie B dimension to the realm of the adult Western. Perhaps Mann's finest Western, 1950's *Winchester '73* introduces the formula that will change a genre forever. James Stewart, just as John Wayne would do six years later in *The Searchers*, reinvented his Western hero persona in hues of dense gray. No longer the gosh-wow polite hero of *Destry Rides Again*, Stewart's portrayal of Lin McAdam starts out saddle-weary, dusty and burned out (not only by the sun), riding with his dedicated friend, trying to track down the murderer of his father. The killer is none other than his own brother, who now calls himself Dutch Henry Brown (Stephan McNally), a cold-blooded outlaw who shot his father in the back. Brothers find one another in Dodge City, marshaled by legendary Wyatt Earp, and both men compete in a rifle-shooting contest to win a special edition of the rifle that won the west... the Winchester '73. At this point in the story, the viewer realizes that both men have a past and that each hates the other, but the other details are forthcoming. The suspenseful shooting contest comes down to a draw, with Lin narrowly beating out Dutch, but Dutch and his men hide in Lin's hotel room, beat him to a pulp and steal the rifle, high-tailing it out of Dodge.

Interestingly, this tense 20-minute sequence is among the

best in a movie that showcases several equally effective moments. The plot's focus expands to show how the rifle brings bloodshed to the many different people who covet this "one of a kind" rifle. They will only possess it for a brief time, before losing it to violence. Basically, the plot develops (again like *The Searchers*) with two men on a journey to recover the rifle and for Lin to kill Dutch for the murder of his father. However, the rifle's trek is just as important a story thread, demonstrating how it brings out the best and worst in mankind and becomes the impetus, similar to the function of the gold in *Treasure of the Sierra Madre*, to that film's dramatic action.

Director Anthony Mann's movies are distinctly quirky in tone and characterization, and here he presents a vision of James Stewart as the tainted, haunted and obsessed hero. Most interestingly, Dan Duryea portrays perhaps the film's most interesting character, Waco Johnny Dean, the crazed outlaw that Dutch is hoping to meet up with to orchestrate their next stagecoach robbery. As portrayed by Duryea, Waco is a Dandy, a sophisticated criminal whose cold-blooded stare implies he will do whatever it takes to get what he wants. He will gun down women, the law and innocent men, always polite and smiling. But the beast is never far from the surface. A pretty Shelley Winters portrays the love interest, the woman who plans to marry a tainted coward who is ultimately slain by Waco. When Lin finally catches up to her at the end, seemingly to win her heart, she states she guesses she loved her fiancée, but his loss is nothing to make her too upset. Mann loves to populate his movies with characters who are amoral, morally bankrupt or at least tainted with sin. For 93 minutes *Winchester '73* soars and becomes one of the most important and enjoyable of the modern Westerns. Extras include an audio interview with James Stewart and trailers. But most impressive is the quality of this high-grain black and white 35mm movie. Seldom have I seen a print this sharp where images in the background are fully in focus. The film is beautifully photographed as well. But in the recent "Universal Western Collection," *Winchester '73* should very well, the first film to purchase.

The Private Life of Sherlock Holmes
Movie: 3.5; Disc: 3.5
[MGM DVD]

Released in a heavily edited version to theaters in 1970, *The Private Life of Sherlock Holmes* was both critically praised and damned, even the arch supporters citing director Billy Wilder's declining artistic powers due to age as excuse to justify the movie's shortcomings. In this expensive-looking production co-scripted by collaborator I.A.L. Diamond, Wilder casts relative unknowns Robert Stephens as Holmes and Colin Blakely as Watson, in a period piece production with dense musical score by Miklos Rozsa. All the ingredients were gathered including a plot that covered lots of different locations and a movie filled with detailed set decoration. However, the movie was not commercially successful upon its release and it is generally considered proof that Billy Wilder was, artistically, over the hill.

However, as reconstructed on DVD, *The Private Life of Sherlock Holmes* is revealed to be an artistic triumph, a movie that while not based upon any specific story by Arthur Conan Doyle is in fact faithful to the author and his literary superstars. The theatrically released film, fairly long at just over two hours, was actually cut by perhaps 55 minutes, as the film was intended by Wilder to be three hours long. Shamefully, the cut sequences are considered to be lost, but MGM did

Colin Blakely and Robert Stephens as Watson and Holmes in *The Private Life of Sherlock Holmes*.

the next best thing. A team of restorationists found audio soundtracks, movie stills, brief movie clips and the actual shooting script to recreate all the missing sequences. As the archival team states, every one of the cut sequences was intended to reveal something fresh about either Holmes or Watson or demonstrate some new aspect of their relationship as lifelong friends. Even with segues to a written script or reconstructing a sequence with still photos, the richness and depth of those excised sequences only demonstrate the travesty that was committed when the film was butchered by the studio and released in truncated form. No doubt about it, the three-hour version of the movie is vastly superior.

Special mention must be made of Christopher Lee's performance as Sherlock's brother Mycroft. In 1970 Christopher Lee was still starring as Dracula in Hammer productions, and *The Private Life of Sherlock Holmes* was perhaps his most important breakout performance and one that demonstrated Lee's expertise transcended the horror cinema. Also, it was the only modern performance that Lee essayed without a hairpiece, but balding or not, the sophisticated rascal still demonstrates his formal good looks and commanding screen presence.

Interestingly, it is the character of Holmes that is most refreshing, his addiction to opium becoming one of the film's principal focal points. As portrayed by Robert Stephens, Sherlock Holmes is a haunted and flawed genius, a man who is both protected and supported by Blakely's Watson, who is portrayed as being almost as clever as Holmes, in the binding friendship that exists between the men. The actual release print used, widescreen and enhanced for 16:9 monitors, is in fabulous condition, letterboxed, with a strong soundtrack. While not a Billy Wilder classic on the same level as his best films of the 1950s and 1960s, *The Private Life of Sherlock Holmes* is here revealed to be an even better film than the one released in 1970, demonstrating one more time how important the DVD medium is for the preservation of films.

Bob Hope:
The Road Show Series Box Set
Road to Singapore: 2.5
Road to Zanzibar: 3.0
Road to Morocco: 2.5
Road to Utopia: 3.0
[Discs: 3.5]
[Universal]

Bob Hope and Bing Crosby became America's beloved comedy team with their series of four Road movies, produced between 1940 and 1945. Even though the series became top-grossers, the duo's comic repartee is always smile inducing and at times howlingly hysterical, but the material generally always lets them down. It becomes apparent that Hope and Crosby are ad-libbing their way through most of this zaniness, and the bare-bones plot becomes little more than an excuse for escapist fun as all the exotic locations were filmed on Hollywood back lots. Even though the character names change (Josh and Ace; Chuck and Fearless; Jeff and Orville; Duke and Chester), the basic comedic relationship remains the same: Hope's characters are always the more cowardly ones, creating personas that are more sympathetic than the harder-edged Crosby. However, while the Crosby character seems to always cheat the Hope character, in a very subtle manner, the Hope character always manages to do the same for Crosby. Crosby generally portrays the con artist out to chisel the public using Hope as his patsy (whether having him collect sucker's money while hidden underneath a magician's table in *Road to Utopia* or being fired out of a carnival cannon in *Road to Zanzibar*), but ultimately the boys

Mad About Movies 4   73

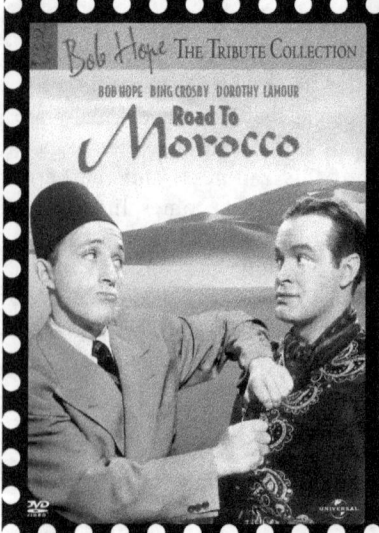  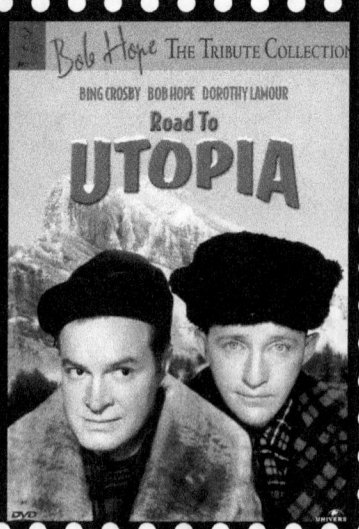

slip up and the jig is up and Hope and Crosby must sneak aboard a ship or escape the country, always just by the skin of their teeth.

In the first three Road pictures, released in 1940, 1941 and 1942 respectively, Dorothy Lamour plays the exotic and skimpily clad island lady, sometimes the innocent victim (Mima, from *Road to Singapore*, who performs with Anthony Quinn, as her dominating partner who is master of the whip) but sometimes also the con artist (along with Una Merkel performing as shady entertainers from Brooklyn who try to seduce money from the boys). However, by movie's end Crosby generally gets the girl Lamour and Hope gets to survive one more day. Strangely, in the final Road movie, *Road to Utopia* released in 1945, three years after the third entry, Dorothy Lamour plays a fully-dressed saloon singer in Alaska, perhaps realizing her sarong-playing roles were over. However, while Lamour offers romantic interest and eye-candy appeal, her performances are adequate at best and she fails to add any exceptional element to the proceedings.

These four road pictures show Hope at his verbal comedic best, and perhaps the final entry, *Road to Utopia*, with onscreen narration by comedian Robert Benchley, becomes the finest entry by nature of its quirky and surreal shenanigans. In one sequence Hope looks up when Crosby points out a mountain, and the screen is filled with the Paramount logo. Hope screams, all he sees is "bread and butter." The framing story used in *Utopia* has the movie open and close with the three stars looking old, 35 years after the adventure in the primary story. Hope and Crosby look dapper and sophisticated, but Lamour simply looks too heavily hidden under gobs of makeup. The payoff comes at the very end when married Lamour and Hope (yes, he won the girl in this one) show Crosby their son... a spitting image of Crosby! Hope wisecracks to the camera: "We adopted him" as the end credits flash on screen.

In films such as *Ghost Breakers*, *My Favorite Brunette* and *Cat and the Canary*, Bob Hope proves he works best as a solo act (along with strong comic support such as Willie Best), but these *Road* movies demonstrate his ability to verbally dazzle with comedic barbs, physically excel at slapstick, perform a quaint soft-shoe and sing a song. Hope is the whole package, and while none of the four films stand out by themselves, the camaraderie of Hope and Crosby still manage to delight 60 years later. All four films feature pristine prints that are flawless, a documentary commemorating the *Road* movies, and shorts featuring Bob Hope such as *Hollywood Victory Caravan*, *Command Performance 1944* and *1945*, and footage of Hope entertaining the troops during WWII. Trailers and photo galleries are also included. For a pleasant afternoon, grab any one of these movies and be prepared to be entertained!

The Far Country
Movie: 3.0; Disc: 3.0
[Universal DVD]

In 1950 *Winchester '73* started a new kind of Western series; quirky Anthony Mann directing James Stewart in A/B productions scored by Joseph Gershenson that sound more than a little like their science fiction counterparts released during the same period of time. And what is most interesting for fans of James Stewart, in these Mann-directed Westerns, is that Stewart plays against his usual type of shy, kindly and delightfully daffy character. In *Winchester '73*, Stewart was obsessed with gunning down his brother, the man who murdered their father. However, four years later, in 1954's *The Far Country*, Stewart's character Jeff has embraced the dark side of human nature even more. The Technicolor CinemaScope

movie (unfortunately, not enhanced for 16:9 monitors; however, the Tech print used, while a tad on the dark side, is breathtaking, with its location snow-covered mountain sequences) begins with Stewart and partner Walter Brennan driving their cattle on a river boat, as Stewart is accused of murdering two men by two shady cowhands whose guns were returned minutes earlier by a very cautious Stewart. As the ship officials prepare to arrest Jeff, Jeff is hidden inside the stately cabin of Mrs. Castle (Ruth Roman); to protect him she strips down to her bra and pretends to make love to her hidden partner. Of course it is Stewart, who is lying beside her in bed.

While the ship officials try to overcharge Walter Brennan for the cattle, the formerly hidden Stewart, on horseback, rushes the cattle off to safety, but unfortunately Brennan, Stewart and the cattle wind up in Skagway, a small frontier town that cattlemen must pass through on their way to Canada. John McIntire rules with an iron fist becoming the town's judge, jury and executioner, all carried out with a smirk and a warped sense of humor (reflecting the off-kilter characterization in a typical Anthony Mann movie). In one smack of the gavel, McIntire takes all Stewart's cattle and charges him $200 for supplies and food—each man leaving must have $100 of supplies (Stewart has only $50). Yet the loner Stewart portrays is also wily and manages to accept a job trailblazing for the Ruth Roman character, whose money controls the town. He also manages to steal back his cattle. McIntire chases him to the Canadian border, vowing he will hang him on his return trip when he must again pass through Skagway.

Stewart's misanthropic character Jeff, besides being a loner, does not trust anyone nor does he particularly like mankind. He is befriended by a young energetic French girl he calls Freckle Face (played by Corrine Calvert), who pays for her doctor father to study advanced medicine in Europe by controlling the sawdust concession in the Dawson saloon. Dawson is a potential Canadian town-to-be, which is inhabited by grizzled gold miners and other independent sorts. All the miners come there to drink and sometimes spill a tad of gold dust on the floor. The clever and patient Freckle Face sifts through the sawdust to find bits of gold that she amasses. Youthful and perky, she falls for the brooding Jeff and constantly tells him he has to help other people, to be kind, to go out of his way for others. Jeff, old and sullen beyond his years, pats her on the head and states when she gets older she will understand a person must look out only for him or herself. When Ruth Roman and John McIntire move into Dawson and set up their own rival restaurant/saloon, McIntire's men boldly steal the gold-mining claims of the residents and ritually slaughter anyone who protests. The town looks to Jeff to become the law, to stand up to these hoodlums, but he has other plans, to sneak back across the American border bypassing Swagway by building a raft and sailing down the

Mad About Movies 4 75

river. However, when the Walter Brennan character shoots his mouth off one time too many, the lovable loudmouth is violently gunned down at the river, and Jeff is shot three times, one in his gun hand, rendering him a cripple. But the clever Jeff has a few tricks up his sleeve, which are revealed during the explosive climax.

While *The Far Country* looks fabulous as photographed in brilliant Technicolor hues with a superb print to match, the dramatic tension is not up to the standards of *Winchester '73*, although the film comes mighty close. Stewart's morally ambiguous leading role is always interesting, and the support provided by McIntire and the rest entertains the audience. Walter Brennan plays, well, Walter Brennan, but his role as the conscience of Jeff ("Jeff, that is simply wrong, that's not right of you") helps define the demons lurking deep within the tainted cowboy hero. The violent ambushing of both Jeff and the Brennan character goes far beyond the B cowboy production expectations for 1954, and it is apparent that the adult Western was already maturing. For fans of Anthony Mann, adult Westerns and James Stewart, *The Far Country* offers a feast of artistic delights.

Mildred Pierce
Movie: 3.5; Disc: 3.5
[Warner Home Video]

If anyone wanted to finally prove that film noir is an attitude, an artistic style and not a genre, one need look no farther than 1945's *Mildred Pierce*, a film noir masterpiece directed by Michael Curtiz. Ernest Haller's cinematography is textbook noir, with dark shadows tracing the motion of characters who walk up stairs, enter brightly lit rooms, drive in the rain, walk on the beach, etc. But if a film noir ever could be considered a woman's picture, with the chief conflict being a class struggle between the *nouveau riche* and old money, *Mildred Pierce* again would be that picture.

By 1945 Joan Crawford was an established star but her career was waning, and her characterization of the title character is among the actress' best work, earning her a Best Actress Academy Award nomination, as a middle-class woman forced to accept a job as a waitress. Before long she has opened her first restaurant which she soon builds into a franchise. All this for her two children, one of whom dies at a young age from pneumonia, the other the vision of sizzling sexuality, a demon child to whom Mildred is willing to give everything. She even marries a parasitic playboy, greasily played by Zachary Scott, in order to provide the type of affluent life her sexpot daughter craves. Ann Blyth has never been better as the spoiled brat

Zachary Scott and Joan Crawford in a publicity shot of *Mildred Pierce*

daughter, who is having an affair with Mildred's playboy husband. In the first scenes of the movie (before flashbacks show the audience what led to the murder), Zachary Scott is brutally shot to death, his last word being "Mildred." Even though Mildred Pierce appears to be the vile murderess, by the movie's shocking finale Mildred again is revealed to be the long-suffering victim, a mother who can protect her daughter in every way except one.

The movie's glittering cinematography (by Ernest Haller) shines, as does its wealth of inspired supporting performances: Jack Carson as the unsophisticated businessman who orchestrates Mildred's rise in the business world (and professes his desire to marry her), but also a ruthless man who sells her out by the end of the movie; Zachary Scott as the wealthy man who never worked a day in his life, but a man whose fortunes are failing and is in constant need of money from

George Raft, Ann Sheridan and Humphrey Bogart in *They Drive by Night*

Mildred in order to survive; Ann Blyth (so sexy) as the daughter from hell who deserves the full wrath of a closet-full of wire hangers; Eve Arden as Mildred's business associate, a crusty dame who might be the only person who truly cares about Mildred.

The original source material used for this Warner Bros. DVD release is absolutely pristine and features intense blacks and perfect contrast. A TCM documentary is included, *Joan Crawford: The Ultimate Movie Star*, as well as a slew of Crawford theatrical movie trailers. I was thoroughly entertained by this gripping noir character study, but people who generally do not like film noir, people who might enjoy *The Little Foxes* or *Now, Voyager*, will probably find *Mildred Pierce* to be their favorite noir, for its insight into the corrupted human psyche is told from a woman's point of view, which makes the movie quite unique.

They Drive By Night
Movie: 3.0; Disc: 3.5
[Warner Home Video]

In 1940, Humphrey Bogart was one year away from breaking through to Hollywood stardom, but here he portrays second banana brother to star George Raft. The movie combines elements of the emerging film noir genre with social drama. Bogart and Raft play independent truckers who are getting squeezed from all angles. They break down along a lonely highway and walk to a truck stop to call their boss to wire them the money to get a wheel fixed. Instead the oily boss sends another trucker to take their load, leaving them without the means of having their vehicle fixed. Also, to rub salt into the wound, the boss tips off the repo man that now is the time to repossess the crippled truck. In another sequence, after the brotherhood of roadside truckers has been established, one man, only desiring to flop into his own bed and cuddle with his wife, drives late at night without benefit of sleep and falls asleep at the wheel. Raft and Bogart, their truck riding behind the truck in distress, try everything they can to alert the sleeping driver. Bogart even volunteers to jump aboard the truck if Raft pulls close enough. However, before the driver can be roused, the truck goes off the road and burns at the bottom of an embankment. Raft and Bogart still attempt a rescue, but the fuel from the truck ignites and explodes. With Raoul Walsh's intense direction featuring spooky nighttime photography, the film's message is clear... independent truckers do not get paid well, they are constantly being cheated by employers and they are forced to overwork to the extent that they fall asleep at the wheel. Bogart himself becomes a victim when the truck he is driving crashes and he loses an arm. In these first-half sequences, feisty Ann Sheridan, portraying a

streetwise truck stop waitress who delivers some quick-witted sarcastic dialogue, befriends George Raft and they slowly fall in love.

But the film's second half evolves into something approximating the soon-to-emerge film noir style where George Raft decides to manage a fleet of trucks owned by friend and former trucker Alan Hale. The problem is Hale's wife, played by newly emerging star Ida Lupino, who only loves her husband for his money and has the hots for George Raft, the man she desires. In a marvelous sequence the wife abandons her husband in his still-running car inside their home garage, where he dies of carbon monoxide poisoning, leaving Lupino's character a free woman. However, in a well-acted courtroom sequence, Lupino cracks on the stand and seems haunted by the fear of returning to her home's garage and facing all her sins. Her vision of insanity is not subtle, yet it is highly effective and creates a shattered persona in direct contrast to Lupino's formerly steely femme fatale bombshell.

The 35mm original source material is pristine with strong contrast. Extras include a featurette about the making of the film, a vintage musical short and a theatrical trailer. *They Drive by Night* is hardhitting and intense, and the performances of Raft, Bogart, Lupino and Sheridan, framed by a tough-as-nails plot and inventive, moody photography make it one of the unsung treasures of 1940s cinema.

Whale Rider
[Special Edition]
Movie: 2.5;
Disc: 3.0
[Columbia/
TriStar Home Video]

Of late two powerful forces have indoctrinated the arts: the independent production and the multicultural sense of The World. *Whale Rider*, one of the most popular independently produced movies released in the United States in 2003, is a rather interesting movie that never quite lives up to its reputation. The New Zealand production deals with a Maori village comprising is- landers who originally settled from Hawaii and whose mystical mythos from the past drives them in modern times. The film starts out as a young tribal woman giving birth to twins struggles for her life. She ultimately succumbs, as does the male twin; only the baby girl survives. In this culture, the male means everything and the at-birth death of the heir apparent is a major blow to the tribe and the girl's father (who loses one child and wife at the same time) and tribal titular leader, the baby's grandfather (who will raise the child when the father, an artist, emigrates to Europe to pursue his art career, forsaking the tribal ways).

Young Keisha Castle-Hughes, portraying the surviving female twin now 12 years old, is the reason the film resonates. Her childish face, on the verge of maturation into womanhood, is ready to assume adult tribal responsibilities, such as a rigorous training period, conducted by her grandfather, involving rituals of rites of passage. The enthusiastic Paikea (Castle-Hughes) is encouraged by her grandmother

Keisha Castle-Hughes in *Whale Rider*

Whale Rider features a wonderful 16:9 widescreen print and the following extras: deleted scenes, director commentary, theatrical trailer and TV spots, a making-of featurette, art and photo gallery, etc. The movie, for the most part, is quirky and leisurely paced, but the performance of Keisha Castle-Hughes, with her quiet determination and longing to be accepted by her cranky grandfather, makes an otherwise adequate movie memorable by nature of this intense and compassionate performance.

to seek training help from her uncle, as her grandfather always belittles her efforts, accusing her of shaming tribal customs. However, at every opportunity, her prowess proves far superior to the other male adolescent trainees (Paikea is superior wielding her dow and she is able to find the whale's tooth necklace dropped into the sea by the grandfather and supposedly to be retrieved by the most worthy of the male warriors-to-be).

At the film's conclusion beached whales lay dying unable to move on the shore. The tribe works day and night to keep them alive and to attempt to push them into the sea, during high tide, with the aid of rope and manpower. However, it is the fearless Paikea who mounts the largest whale and literally rouses the beast to muster the strength to ride out into the sea, with Paikea on top. As the whale skims the surface of the water and swims underneath, we see the little girl maintain her poise as the mammal descends. Only hours later is the near-dead body of the girl found and all the whales have returned to the sea. In the movie's emotional finale, a boat started but never finished by Paikea's father is finally made seaworthy. Paikea and her grandfather proudly sail out to sea, accompanied by the warrior-males of the tribe. The young girl's destiny of leading her people to new times following the old ways is fulfilled.

The Adventures of Robin Hood
Movie: 3.5; Disc: 4.0
[Warner Home Video]

Amazingly, action-adventure used to mean epic scope, ensemble acting, and a detailed plotted script and dynamic star turn performances. When viewed by today's young audiences, the 1938 classic *The Adventures of Robin Hood* might seem quaint and almost leisurely paced, but this Michael Curtiz–directed classic still holds up superbly, even if judged by this current generation of jaded eyes. With an all-star cast including Errol Flynn, Olivia de Havilland, Basil Rathbone and Claude Rains, the movie is magically enhanced by the exquisite Technicolor photography. While the remastered three-strip Technicolor appears slightly muted in contrast and tone, the flesh tones are perfect and the color overall is superb.

The heroic performance delivered by Errol Flynn is movie magic, with his playful roguishness contrasted by his commitment to helping the downtrodden. Flynn can play the romantic, the wily sarcastic pest, the acrobatic fencing dynamo or the practical joker; thus his Robin Hood is multidimensional. His rapport with the ensemble cast of Merry Men (including Alan Hale, Eugene Pallette, etc.) furthers the concept of male bonding and creates a brethren of feisty male warriors who fight hard and play even harder. And when it comes to villainy, *The Adventures of Robin Hood* offers a double-dose of classic screen evil. We have the interim king played by Claude Rains, a very prissy and effeminate man who is dastardly and devious and not to be trusted. Alongside comes the dashing and daring Basil Rathbone, masculine and evil, one of the cinema's most masterful swordsmen, whose duel with Flynn becomes a centerpiece of the entire movie. In fact, the movie's climactic finale features chandelier swinging and jumping from high stone staircases all set off nicely by one of the best sword fights in movie history.

Even though *The Adventures of Robin Hood* was produced over 60 years ago, the film's sense of romance, adventure, indignation and the positive will of the people survive loud and clear, demonstrating that the adventure genre need not depend upon special effects or nonstop kinetic pacing. And where today can we find stars that radiate the charisma of Errol Flynn, Basil Rathbone or Claude Rains? Thus *The Adventures Robin Hood* may be old in years, but when it comes to maintaining a vitality and creative spark, the movie is as young as it ever was.

This stellar DVD two-disc set features a pristine 35mm remastering of the original movie in Dolby 5.1 surround with close to Technicolor saturation, but the extras are worthy of the price. We have audio commentary, an isolated musical track, the *Warner Night at the Movies* shorts including a musical short subject, a cartoon and theatrical trailer. We also have a featurette about the film's production, brief outtakes and studio blooper reel, rare home movies shot by Basil Rathbone on the set, two Warner Bros. Robin Hood–inspired cartoons: *Rabbit Hood* and *Robin Hood Daffy*, a Robin Hood radio show broadcast, a documentary on Technicolor and production details. As fantastic as the presentation of the movie becomes, the extras go the extra distance to make this a definitive collection of a classic movie. This is a got-to-own package!

The Italian Job
Movie: 3.0; Disc: 3.5
[Paramount Home Video]

The caper movie has always been one of the more intelligent adult film genres, and while this type of movie has languished for a while, movies such as *Heist* and Steven Soderbergh's *Ocean's Eleven* brought this genre back into the limelight. Now F. Gary Gray's *The Italian Job* continues the resurgence. *The Italian Job* definitely recalls the slightly superior *Ocean's Eleven* remake, but it is still marvelously intelligent entertainment. Less breezy and heavier in tone than *Ocean's Eleven*, *The Italian Job* features a marvelous ensemble cast featuring Mark Wahlberg, Charlize Theron, Edward Norton, Mos Def, Seth Green and Donald Sutherland. Amazingly, the film's opening heist involves a heavy metal safe falling through several floors of a building and supposedly landing in a

speed boat (when actually it falls underwater in Venice); the chase is on as the Russian Mafia chases the fleeing boat, acting as decoy, while underwater scuba divers are carefully stealing gold bars from the now-open safe. The pacing, cinematography and incredibly executed stunts only enhance the sense of fun until the merry group of pranksters are escaping and sharing stories about how they will spend their share of the money. Old pro Sutherland loves young newcomer Wahlberg, commending him for the intelligence employed stealing the money without using a gun or weapon of any type. It is apparent that Sutherland looks to Wahlberg as a surrogate son, since he has all but deserted his lovely daughter Theron. [SPOILER ALERT] Then in a sudden surprise, it turns out that just too quiet Edward Norton sold out his friends, with his gang cutting off the escape vehicle upon a high bridge. Norton's gang attempts to slaughter Sutherland's gang with automatic gunfire while the escape vehicle plunges into the chilly water below. Most emotionally painful is the horrible death of Donald Sutherland, who dies in Wahlberg's arms.

The movie's plot moves several months ahead with Wahlberg concocting a new scheme to get his bounty back, this time using Theron as the safe expert (like father like daughter). The setup again is beautiful, but just before the scheme can be executed, Theron inadvertently tips off Norton that she is in fact Sutherland's daughter by using an odd phrase that he used to use. From this point on, the audience thinks the jig is up, but Wahlberg challenges Norton to figure out the scheme and to hold on to his gold. Before the movie ends, even more twists and turns occur, the final one involving the returning Russian Mafia and a stellar chase with mini-European cars. The movie itself is thoroughly entertaining and filled with surprise upon surprise, until the audience doesn't know what will happen next and what other jolts will follow. Just when the audience thinks they have it all figured out, guess what, they don't! Again, the plot is brought to life with an amazing ensemble cast that just sparkles. For adults who enjoy a thought-provoking thriller, *The Italian Job* more than meets the bill.

Extras on the Special Edition DVD set include documentaries about both making the movie and transforming the words on the page to the screen. Other documentaries are included about the creation of the stunts, the mighty mini-car races, deleted scenes, trailer, etc. All in all, it's a pretty impressive package.

Seabiscuit
Movie: 3.5; Disc: 3.5
[Dreamworks DVD]

Seabiscuit is Hollywood movie-making of the most inspired sort, doing nearly the impossible: maintaining viewer interest for almost two and a half hours by focusing on a team of broken-down people placing their hopes and dreams on the back of a broken-down horse. The movie's frame is a snappy voiceover narration as delivered by a noted historian, David McCullough, creating the history of Seabiscuit as metaphor for Depression-era America. In fact *Seabiscuit* is successful because the story becomes a metaphor for America. People broken, people disheartened, people riddled by a changing American landscape all brought together to achieve their individual dreams by transforming a horse that is considered too small to achieve greatness into the greatest racehorse of all time.

Director Gary Ross' style is utterly amazing. In two sequences he truncates essential data into something bite-size yet emotionally heartfelt, allowing time to focus on the aspects he feels needs to be illuminated in more depth. The first truncated sequence is the automobile death and funeral of Jeff Bridges' son, and we do not even get a flash of a collision or a sub-woofered intensified thud of screeching brakes or the bang of metal on metal. Very subtle and very effective. The other truncated sequence is the courtship and marriage of Bridges to his new wife. Again, little time is wasted yet the plot is forwarded and clearly explained.

The aspect that is emphasized is the budding relationship between jockey Tobey Maguire, businessman Jeff Bridges and lonesome cowboy trainer Chris Cooper. And once the horse is introduced, we have the glue that holds this ramshackle family together. Bridges becomes the huckster who sells the story of Seabiscuit to America, literally forcing a race with the champion racehorse from the

Tobey Maguire as Red Pollard in *Seabiscuit*

East Coast who is avoiding this wonder-horse from the West. Cooper becomes the taciturn trainer who understands the psychology of horses better than he understands the psyches of human beings, and he uses this knowledge to have jockey Maguire become one with the horse. And Maguire, deserted by his family at a racetrack when the jockey was in his mid-teens, finds in Bridges the father, home and family he never had and the potential to achieve the dream of a lifetime.

The dominating theme of the movie is being battered and abused yet still having the courage to come back, to keep trying. America herself has been battered by the Depression, Bridges has been battered by the loss of a son and a divorce resulting from that loss, Cooper is the battered cowboy loner who fears the end of the wilderness with man losing his grip with nature and Maguire is the battered child who literally lives by his wits (being a jockey, being a poor boxer). And poor Seabiscuit, the most battered character of all, the offspring of Man-O-War, who is declared inferior from the get-go, and is confined to running the lowest echelon of horse races. So in the best spirit of America, when that awkward little horse wins we all win. That horse helped lift America's spirits from defeat during the Depression, and Seabiscuit's wins became symbolic for much, much more than merely a horserace.

Quite simply *Seabiscuit* is one of the finest movies released in 2003, and as captured on DVD with a superior widescreen print and a Dolby 5.1 soundtrack, the movie looks and sounds as good at home as it did at the movies. Extras include documentaries and interviews with the book's author and movie's director. For a movie that moves at a leisurely clip, its emotional resonance is quite profound.

A Mighty Wind
Movie: 3.0; Disc: 3.5
[Warner Home Video]

Satires only work when viewers understand the topics being satirized. For me *Best in Show* left me cold, while many friends went into hysterics, because I always felt that prissy dog shows were hilarious in the first place. A movie that mocks their seriousness goes over my own head because the actual thing is hilarious by itself.

Now director-writer Christopher Guest and actor-writer Eugene Levy turn their critical eye to the world of late 1950s/early 1960s folksingers and make fun of musical acts such as Peter, Paul and Mary, The New Christy Minstrels and Ian and Sylvia. First of all, to add a little history, the folk music created by these and other acts was homogenized, urban sanitized versions of the rawer original music, captured and brought to the masses by folk musicologist Harry Smith in his landmark *Anthology of American Folk Music* released in 1952 (Smith assembled obscure 78s released from 1927-1935). Hip college students and music shop aficionados immediately took to this outside-the-box raw American roots music and tried to approximate it in rather overly serious and too meticulous urbanized musical settings which became the era of The Kingston Trio, The Weavers (the most authentic of the batch), The Limelighters, etc.

Thus, the Mary-less (Peter, Paul and Mary-esque) Folkmen just have that doe-eyed blissful face of wonderment that seems so perfect (the movie's coda, where bass-playing balding male becomes blonde-haired masculine woman is hysterical… the act finally has created its "Mary"!). Eugene Levy's Mitch of Mitch and Mickey is perhaps just a tad too psychedelic and crispy for the folk boom era, but his characterization is both bizarre and touching as he wanders aimlessly in the city streets before a reunion TV concert and returns with one beautiful flower to give companion Mickey. The kinky-below-the-surface New Main Street Singers (shades of the New Christy Minstrels) features a rousting family-style hootenanny ensemble that tries just a little too hard to create that squeaky-clean Moral Majority image.

Surprisingly, the all-original folk concoctions, especially the title song "A Mighty Wind," are done straight without even the hint of tongue-in-cheek. Of course I have several friends who think lyrics from the 1960s such as "If I had a hammer, I'd hammer in the morning, I'd hammer in the evening, all over this land" are tongue in cheek. But if you enjoyed such lyrics from the folk craze, the lyrics to these clever acoustic ditties rate right up there with them. The artists, who also composed the music and lyrics, deliver them with conviction, heart and soul, and even they realize such songs can evoke a little bit of humor due to their self-righteous college campus-directed audiences, who took all of this a tad too seriously 40-something years ago.

But what makes *A Mighty Wind* succeed is the heart and soul of the artists who deliver full-bodied human performances. All of them take their art quite seriously, as I am sure all the original artists also did, and their joy over doing this mock reunion concert is an epiphany experience for all their lives. So the movie is not only funny (in the sense that it touches the raw nerves that fueled the original folk movement) but it is also nostalgic and heartwarming.

Besides featuring a wonderful 5.1 Dolby print with excellent soundtrack, the DVD extras include mock bios of the fictitious musical groups, extra concert performances, outtakes, "vintage" TV performances of the bands, an uninterrupted version of the reunion TV concert and audio commentary. Anyone should enjoy this razor-sharp re-investigation of the urban folk resurgence, but to people who remember and enjoyed the real thing, this satiric homage is inspired and touches the heart.

**The Treasure
of the Sierra Madre**
Movie: 3.0; Disc: 4.0
[Warner Home Video]

Tim Holt, Humphrey Bogart and Walter Huston don't need no stinkin' badges in *The Treasure of the Sierra Madre*.

Bravo for Warner Home Video for digging deeply into its classic movie archives. This two-disc set, part of the recently released Bogart Collection, is a film lover's dream come true. The original source material (except for one brief barroom sequence, which appears to have a second-generation look) is absolutely sparkling and pristine, having a dense contrast and fine-grain clarity. The soundtrack is also beefy and robust. Extras include the outstanding *Warner Night at the Movies 1948*, introduced by Leonard Maltin, which features newsreel, Bugs Bunny cartoon, trailer to *Key Largo* and a wonderful comedy short spoofing Phillip "Snarlowe" and Warner detective movies of the time. The second disc features a feature-length documentary on the life and work of director-writer John Huston, a documentary on the production of *The Treasure of the Sierra Madre*, another Bugs Bunny cartoon which spoofs the feature, the Luxe Radio Theatre version (which stars Bogart and Walter Huston) and the Treasure Trove which includes photos, storyboards, publicity material and cast and crew bios. The first disc even features 12 classic Bogart trailers.

But none of this would matter if *The Treasure of the Sierra Madre* wasn't such a classic movie, one of the best John Huston movies and definitely one of the finest Humphrey Bogart performances (along with *In a Lonely Place*). To me I feel both *The Maltese Falcon* and *The Big Sleep* are better movies, but *Treasure of the Sierra Madre* is performance driven, becoming both a quasi-Western and morality tale. Based upon a novel by the reclusive B. Traven, the movie is actually an updating of *The Pardoner's Tale* from Chaucer's *The Canterbury Tales,* where three "rioters" looking to hunt down and slay death during The Black Death era of the Middle Ages, are told by an old man they could find death under an apple tree, but they find only gold coins. Drawing straws, the youngest rioter has to go to town to get supplies and instead poisons two bottles of wine. His two cohorts, guarding the gold, plot to murder the youngest member upon his return. By story's end one man has been stabbed to death and the other two die by drinking poison. Here, Bogart refuses to go to town to get supplies, thinking the other two men (grizzled and elderly Howard, played by director Huston's father Walter; and the youngest Curtin, played by cowboy star Tim Holt) will run off with his gold. The youngest member Curtin gets the nod to travel to town for supplies.

Bogart's performance runs the gamut from down and out laborer who merely wants to collect an honest day's wages, to panhandler who always manages to beg for a handout from the man in the white suit (John Huston himself), to the paranoid man who begins to talk to himself and sleeps with one eye open, to the cold-blooded killer who bets Curtin $105,000 (the stash of all three prospectors) that Curtin will fall asleep before he will, and when that happens, Dobbs gets the jump on the decent Curtin, marches him into the deep brush, and fires two shots to finish him off. If Bogart were to be nominated for an Academy Award, his performance as Fred C. Dobbs is the splashiest one of his career and is certainly Oscar-worthy. Me, I still prefer his private dick roles, but his Dobbs demonstrates the total range of the actor's abilities.

But Walter Huston's off-kilter performance as life-long prospector Howard is the film's standout performance, requiring the actor to speak all his lines of dialogue at super fast speed, dance a jig, laugh hysterically for several minutes and to maintain a keen, perceptive eye on the psychological inner workings of his partners, men he considers decent men right up until the end, stating it was the gold that created the ultimate evil in Dobbs. The manner in which Walter Huston creates a world-weary philosophy, which is still filled with hope for the human species, is rather off-putting and interesting to digest. His performance is always energetic and becomes the glue that holds the three-way ensemble performance together.

For me, *The Treasure of the Sierra Madre* is slightly overlong and sometimes meanders, but at its heart are three of the finest performances in 1940s cinema, and the direction of John Huston is simply superb.

Once Upon a Time in the West
Movie: 3.0; Disc: 4.0
MGM

For me the Western genre peaked with John Ford and Howard Hawks. Movies such as *The Searchers, Red River, Rio Bravo* and *The Man Who Shot Liberty Valance* define what the Western genre has always been capable of producing. The modern Westerns, movies such as *The Wild Bunch* and *Ride the Wild Country* directed by Sam Peckinpah, are a notch below, always trying too hard and deliberately to reconstruct what came so naturally before. And for me, the Westerns of Sergio Leone are quite perplexing. Leone, whose career was an admittedly heroic attempt to redefine those classics of the past, seemed to be creating opera where pop was more appropriate. Both the strengths and the flaws of Leone's moviemaking are clearly on display in what many consider to be his Western masterpiece (others consider *The Good, The Bad and the Ugly* to be his best).

First of all, his homage to those beloved Western sidewinders opens *Once Upon a Time in the West* in classic style, with those well-worn faces of Woody Strode

and Jack Elam lingering in tight close-up trying to keep the flies at bay. Charles Bronson, playing the mysterious stranger that Clint Eastwood had formerly portrayed, is attempting to avenge the brutal hanging of his brother by a gang of thugs, headed by Frank, the most evil performance that Henry Fonda ever committed to movies. Literally the guilt of an older brother's death is placed squarely on the shoulders of Bronson, whose brother stands on his shoulders, a noose tightly wound around his neck. When Bronson's legs finally wear down, he drops his weight and his brother dies. Dribs and drabs of information reveal the stranger's motives for returning as pieces of the puzzle slowly fall into place. This leads to an identification of Leone's chief flaw (and others might say his strength)—his lethargic and leisurely pacing. Once Upon a Time in the West occupies 165 minutes of screen time, and while the plot is complex and the characterizations subtly defined, Leone likes to use his cinematographer to create panoramic sweeps of the landscape, create a mood of arid desolation and the teeming birth of a new city, created by the expansion of the railroad (becoming the defining symbol of the production... where the railroad advances, civilization also advances). Sometimes Sergio Leone's love affair with the camera and the simple look of his Western world takes precedent over both plot and characterization. Whether this is his artistic strength or self-indulgent downfall, the viewer can decide.

But *Once Upon a Time in the West* features several masterful sequences that long linger, especially the tragic slaughter of the frontier family. In a sprawling location shot demonstrating the positioning and actions of all family members, the desert animal noises come to a crashing silence as the father stops in his tracks, freezes, and surveys the landscape, the look in his eyes telegraphing that something is deadly wrong. Soon, from out of nowhere, a piercing crash of a bullet fells the young daughter, who simply drops not knowing what hit her. Then, within seconds, the entire family is gunned down, the sequence being an ideal marriage of sight and sound, with sequences of absolute quiet being punctuated with exploding gun fire that slaughters a family within half a minute. The perpetrators of such violence are not seen until only the youngest son survives, a tear running down his cheek. Then from out of the brush come the stereotypical outlaws wearing their long coats that whip in the breeze. The outlaws approach the young boy, with Henry Fonda's character of Frank slightly smiling, looking toward the boy. When one member of his gang calls him by name, the young boy's fate is sealed, as Fonda takes out his revolver and shots the child at point blank range.

Sequences such as this abound in Leone's loving tribute to the American Western (mostly filmed in Italy but a few sequences of Monument Valley are included), and while the film is epic in scope, the tone sometimes comes off perhaps a tad *too* reverent and self-consciously self-important for its own good. Leone's vision of the American Western as opera is both powerful yet very self-conscious, but sometimes the intensity of Leone's vision produces a fabulous cinematic effect.

The restored widescreen print is breathtaking and enhanced for 16:9 monitors, and the remastered 5.1 Dolby Surround is awesome and works to the film's advantage. This two-disc set features a multitude of extras including a commentary track, three documentaries, production gallery and trailer. And this box set sold for $15 at Best Buy. Besides being one of the most important DVD releases of the past year, it is definitely one of the most affordable.

Melody Ranch
Movie: 2.5; Disc: 3.5
[Image Entertainment]

Gene Autry starred in perhaps, along with Roy Rogers, the best-loved B Western series ever produced. They exist in a childhood world where modern technology (the radio broadcast superstar) meets the Old West, yet this isn't quite the Old West (trolley cars, automobiles are ever visible). In this Gene Autry outré world, the code of the West exists in this modern world of 1940 where even children could believe the Old West still exists in modern America.

Melody Ranch, released in 1940, became a musical extravaganza co-starring Jimmy Durante and Ann Miller (who unfortunately succumbed to lung cancer the very week we previewed the DVD), who steal the show, or at least add some pizzazz and spice to the mix. Gene Autry always spends a good deal of time crooning his country and western tunes, but the urban presence of Durante and Miller put the focus even more on music than gunplay. Thus, while *Melody Ranch* was one of the more popular Autry entries, it might not be a favorite of the kids who expected more focus on fistfights and exploding six-shooters.

The plot is action-packed. Autry, a radio celebrity who works with the flighty Ann Miller, a celebrity who arrives late for her live broadcast and seems to have a lackadaisical attitude, goes with Roy to visit his Western hometown of Torpedo. There he will be honorary sheriff and try to clean up the town that is run by an outlaw gang of brothers (one of whom, Jasper, is played by Universal 1950s contract player Joe Sawyer, who is memorable for his appearance in *It Came from Outer Space*). Miller slowly falls in love with Rogers, coming to understand his good-heartedness and dedication to his townspeople.

George "Gabby" Hayes plays the grizzled second banana sidekick, and the set piece of a trolley train that carries citizens from outside the town into the heart of downtown becomes pivotal during the movie's climax when Autry tries to get the citizenry to vote in an election that is totally controlled by the villains who do not allow everyone to vote. Setting up a town barricade, Autry's trolley comes barreling down the main street, guns blazing, as his men back him up and overthrow the villains that have been holding the town in a grip of terror. Strangely enough, in this surreal world, even the villain's brothers are also singing cowboys who are jealous of Autry's success. What keeps the film energized is the comic support of Jimmy Durante who plays a tenderfoot cowardly cowboy (he's Roy's radio partner) who delivers fractured puns and clever comedic shenanigans with impeccable timing. The best sequences in the movie revolve around Durante. And Miller plays a perky love interest to perfection.

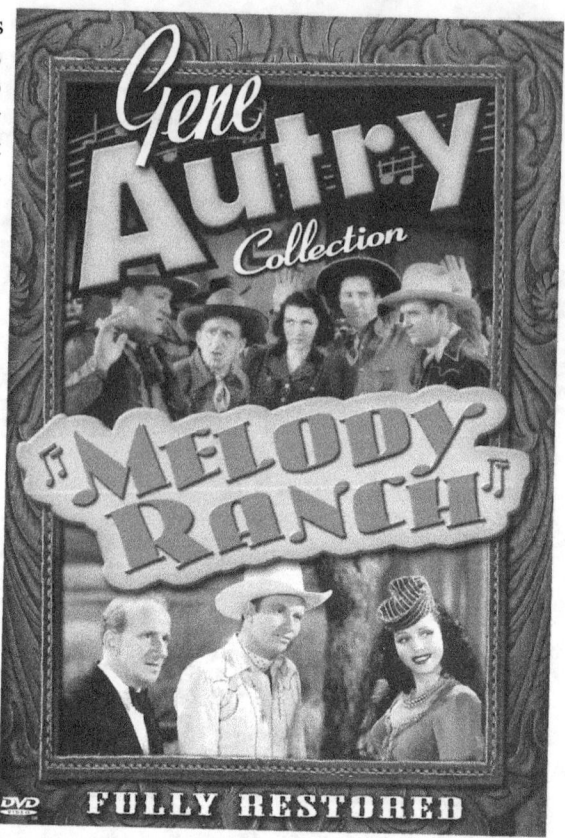

Extras on this disc include Gene Autry and Pat Buttram reminiscing at the Melody Ranch Theatre TV show, and excerpts from the Melody Ranch radio show. Production and publicity still gallery, posters, pressbook and lobby card gallery are included, as are trivia and movie facts. The original source material is exquisite with good contrast and sound. And for all fans of B Westerns and of Durante and Miller, *Melody Ranch* is a B Western favorite worth revisiting.

Swimming Pool (Unrated)
Movie: 2.5; Disc: 3.0
[Focus Features]

One must give *Swimming Pool* a half-point simply on the basis of Ludivine Sagnier's nude sequences, which occur frequently and all so naturally… it's as though the entire world is her private bath and she is comfortable in that natural state. And God, she looks heavenly.

But unfortunately, *Swimming Pool*, as written and directed by Francois Ozon, is akin to watching the dullest film that David Lynch *never* directed. The movie is billed as a thriller, and yes, a grisly murder does occur near the movie's end, but the movie is not a mystery nor is it technically a thriller. To be accurate, it is a psychological probing exploring the processes of a writer's mind and how she creates a quasi world of reality when crafting her art.

The movie's surprise [spoiler ahead] concerns the fact that at movie's end, when the Charlotte Rampling character returns to the city to see her publisher, she passes a young girl who turns out to be the publisher's actual daughter, who is an entirely different girl

popular detective series, but her popularity is being challenged by a new upstart writer who gets her publisher's attention. Frustrated and thinking she is capable of writing something deeper, more personal, the writer is invited to stay at her publisher's secluded French home where she can be alone to write. Before she gets settled, the publisher's daughter arrives unexpectedly and promptly sheds her clothes and romps nude in and around the pool, brings a different man home every night (most of whom are much older than she) and has wild sex, the two women rubbing each other the wrong way. Until the two slowly become friends and bond, which leads to the sexy daughter befriending a waiter that the Rampling character takes a fancy to, and after almost joining in as a threesome of wild partying, the Rampling character instead goes off to bed. And while the other two frolic in the pool, the night ends with the man viciously bludgeoned to death with a rock. The Rampling character helps the weirded-out young girl bury the body and destroy evidence. At one critical point the young girl says, you did not burn all the evidence… you did not burn your book. And with this line, it all made sense.

Since the publisher's daughter and the frolicking tart are not the same, it is obvious that the sex tramp only exists in the Rampling character's repressed mind (as she only seems to condemn the younger's sexual escapades). But it becomes apparent that the Rampling character secretly desires to have wild sex with a different man every night, that she secretly wishes to drink too much and smoke marijuana, that she desires to seduce strange men and feel more comfortable with the public display of her body. At the movie's end, when the younger woman mentions burning the book as evidence, it is apparent that the sexpot only exists in the pages of Rampling's book and that by burning her book, she would destroy all evidence of all people and actions that occurred during her French working vacation.

However, even sweet-young-thing nudity and a twist ending cannot salvage what is otherwise a dull internal character study that lacks mystery, suspense and logic. *Swimming Pool* is an interesting exercise that attempts too deliberately to manipulate the cinematic medium. It is worth one visit or two, but it simply fails to grip its audience. Minimal extras included deleted scenes, a trailer and a DST audio track. But where is the obligatory audio commentary when we really, really need it??!!!

Matchstick Men
Movie: 3.0; Disc: 3.0
[Warner Home Video]

Ridley Scott, in between rousing spectacles such as *Gladiator* and his classic horror opuses *Alien* and *Hannibal*, produces more personal movies from time to time, such as *Matchstick Men*, a cleverly scripted film done in the style of David Mamet's *House of Games*.

Nicolas Cage delivers one of his finest performances yet, as a neurotic con artist who discovers he is the biological father of a 14-year-old girl who desires to bond with dad by learning the ropes of con art-

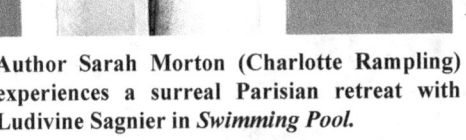

Author Sarah Morton (Charlotte Rampling) experiences a surreal Parisian retreat with Ludivine Sagnier in *Swimming Pool*.

from the "daughter" she shared her adventures with at her publisher's hideaway French house for the past 90 minutes.

Basically, the plot concerns the Rampling character, who writes a

Mad About Movies 4   87

istry! Alison Lohman's free-spirited daughter is played with gusto as she comes between Roy (Cage) and his partner in crime Frank (Sam Rockwell) who feels the little girl will be the cause of errors made. On the one hand we have the concerned and dedicated father (less so at first, but he quickly melts to the charms of his baby girl), but at the same time Roy ruthlessly swindles people out of their money with creative scams that mark him as an artist at his trade (and he takes pride in the fact that he never used a gun nor violence and that people give him their money willingly). However, unless he's on his meds, he suddenly develops eye tics and nervous habits that always threaten to break his character in the middle of a scam, so he has to undergo therapy with a new psychiatrist who feels Roy only *thinks* he needs medication.

The plot gets even more involved with Frank befriending a potential Mafia connection who is ripe for the picking. If the deal goes sour, Roy and Frank will have the wrath of organized crime at their doorsteps. As expected, things do go awry (and of course Roy incorporates his daughter into the con so she is involved as well) and Roy and his daughter are soon on the run facing gunplay and violence for the first time in his career… with his daughter facing the danger as well.

In the best con artist movies, the plot contains twists and turns so that whatever the audience feels is happening is not really happening at all. For me, *Matchstick Men* featured a plot twist so riveting and surprising that I never saw it coming until it exploded all over the screen. The old saying, what goes round comes round, leads to a climax full of surprises. The film, a comedic thriller, is more drama than comedy, and by the final reel, the movie almost becomes tragic, but its lightness of spirit still manages to prevail. To reveal anything about the movie's end would destroy the surprise, so let me end the critique here.

Once again, Cage, Rockwell and Lohman create performances that connect emotionally, even if every relationship created is slightly askew and not quite real. The movie is dependent upon quirky performances and warm interrelationships from which a mighty slick plot develops. Yes, the movie contains a few flaws and it is far from being a classic, but for two hours the movie entertains and touches the heart. Extras include a production-of documentary and a director's how-to documentary, audio commentary and trailer. For an offbeat drama with involving characterizations, *Matchstick Men* holds plenty of surprises.

King of the Royal Mounted
Movie: 3.5; Disc: 3.5
[VCI Entertainment]

I am finding serials later in life, and thanks to excellent packages produced by companies such as VCI, I am discovering new movie entertainment that generally eluded me all these years. It doesn't take long to realize that far too few Republic serials have been released to DVD, and that the year 1940 was a

wonderful time for chapterplays to be produced, especially if the directorial team was William Witney and John English. Zane Grey's *King of the Royal Mounted*, a 12-chapter serial, is not one of the most highly regarded serials (such as *Captain Marvel* and *Drums of Fu Manchu*), but *King of the Royal Mounted* is one of my favorites so far. Here are a few reasons why. First, the Canadian setting is different, for we have a quasi-Western movie setting with horses and shoot-'em-ups, yet the movie is laced more in tall pines bound with rocky cliffs, waterfalls and logs floating down the river. We have French Canadian sneaks and gangs who hang out in log cabins. And instead of the sheriff and his deputies, we have the Royal Mounted Police. The settings vary, from burning forests, a warehouse inferno sequence that is the equivalent of the burning of Atlanta in *Gone with the Wind*, wilderness sequences, underwater submarine sequences, etc. I like the fact that action occurs in rapidly changing locations. Secondly, we have a plot that if filled with multiple villains (Robert Strange as Kettler who works for the Nazis; Bryant Washburn as shifty-eyed Matt Crandall who pretends to be using Compound X for infant paralysis; and Harry Cording as Wade Garson, the serials' most exposed villain who is punched out or captured and always manages to escape to return in the next chapter) that always manage to kick the plot forward. The plot features a marvelous hero (Allan Lane as Dave King), some incredible cliffhangers and several unexpected deaths peppered along the way. In other words, *King of the Royal Mounted* is an exceptional and always entertaining serial featuring villains disguised as police agents, a supposed sanitarium for the sick and paralyzed that is actually the villain's hangout where they ship Compound X out of the country, fistfights that begin when the hero uses his foot to yank the rug and throw gun-wielding villains off balance, secret radio broadcasting units that lie just behind the hidden wood paneling and submarines that use human beings as torpedo missiles that can be shot out of the gates. All pretty amazing stuff, constantly straining credibility, but such incidents are all acceptable in the quasi-real world of the serial.

King of the Royal Mounted is presented with a pristine print that features a dense soundtrack. All 12 chapters appear on one disc and the viewing experience is always first-rate, never wavering, and the story, no matter how silly or ridiculous, captivates the audience's attention. This is one of my favorite serials and is a title I recommend to all lovers of action film cinema, not just serial buffs.

The Green Archer
Movie: 3.5; Disc: 3.5
[VCI Entertainment]

When it comes to serials, generally Republic always reigns on top while Columbia wallows on the bottom. However, thanks to VCI, we can now reexamine the Golden Age serials of James W. Horne (*The Green Archer* and *Captain Midnight*, two of his best). Horne created quirky and off-kilter serials, at times almost seeming to spoof the serial concept. However, to me, Horne's serials always seem to be fun and fast-paced and while little touches of humor abound, they

never interfere with the drama and suspense at hand.

The Green Archer, released during 1940 by Columbia, is one of the finest serials produced, featuring a pint-sized but wiry Victor Jory as dashing hero and leading man, getting into massive fistfights every chapter (and sometimes two or three free-for-alls each chapter). Would it be wishing for too much if Jory used his gun a tad more frequently to dispatch members of the gang that literally beat him up multiple times during the serial? Jory, playing an insurance investigator, is fearless, energetic and crafty, yet he manages to end up in all the wrong places at the wrong times. Equally impressive is gentleman gangster James Craven, whose distinguished graying hair and mustache defy the fact that he is ruthless and cold blooded. Villain Craven frames his brother Michael, who is on board a sabotaged train, on his way to prison, and when the train crashes, Craven's character of Bellamy takes over the ancestral castle, Garr Castle, which he uses as his center of operations for his outlaw gang. At Garr Castle hidden rooms abound and every room appears to have a secret entrance. Snooping relatives of Michael are captured and held prisoner in the castle with Spike Holland (Jory) aware of Bellamy's evil operations but unable to do anything about it. Soon even the police suspect Holland of criminal intentions and he has to evade both Bellamy's crime syndicate and the men in blue. Thrown into the mix is the mythic Green Archer who is said to haunt Garr Castle, and this mysterious, silent Robin Hood–type hero always appears just in the nick of time to rescue Holland or one of the women in distress, and then disappear just as suddenly. To confuse matters, one of Bellamy's thugs, Bret (Jack Ingram), also dresses up as The Green Archer (looking exactly the same as the real McCoy). So we literally have one heroic archer and one evil one, and things get pretty frantic when one of Bellamy's gang says hello to Bret when it's really the actual Green Archer, or the gang thinks they have their hands on the real archer, beat him up, only to have a pissed-off Bret emerge with a black eye.

The voiceover narration at chapter ends, previewing next week's chapter, constantly warns the audience to keep an eye on the butler and other shifty types, constantly planting suspicions and creating slews of red herrings. Unfortunately, Bellamy may be a villain larger than life, but his death sequence is almost an afterthought. A policeman orders him to stop, and when he does not, the policeman shoots him dead, but the cinematographer shows the policeman firing rather than focusing upon the villain dying. This is the biggest disappointment of the entire serial, which is otherwise quite exciting and thrill packed. From the cliff-hanging train wreck at the end of chapter one, to the drowning chambers, to a roomful of knives descending from the ceiling, director James W. Horne keeps the story fast-paced and offers plenty of surprises (especially the revelation of the Green Archer's identity). *The Green Archer*, while not a Republic serial, is one of the best serials Columbia ever produced and its pristine delivery by VCI invites a first-time viewing or a revisiting.

Captain Midnight
Movie: 3.5; Disc: 3.5
[VCI Entertainment]

James W. Horne, still at the peak of his form, returns in 1942 with Columbia's *Captain Midnight*, based upon the popular radio show. While *The Green Archer* was quirky and action-packed, *Captain Midnight* continues with Horne's odd tone and outrageousness that somehow works. In many ways *Captain Midnight* might be superior to *The Green Archer* in that

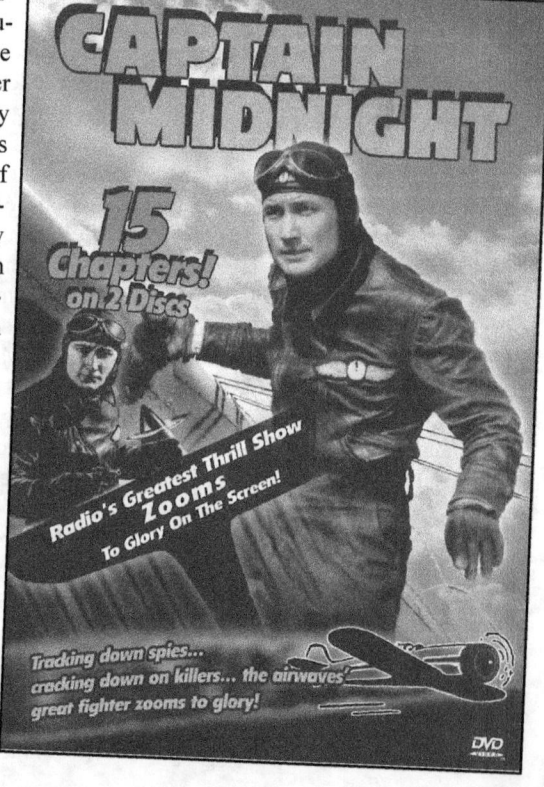

Captain Midnight (Dave O'Brien)

hero Dave O'Brien makes a more believable hero than Victor Jory and leading lady Dorothy Short is one of the feistiest heroines in serial history. Instead of only doing the typical female serial thing, screaming (which Short does do well) and fainting, Short is quite resourceful. In sequences she pushes the villain backward to lock him out, manhandles a hospital nurse employed by the syndicate so she can steal the nurse's uniform and escape—and she can generally out-run, jump fences and race cars equal to her male counterparts. The marvelous James Craven is back as an even more menacing villain, Ivan Shark, who is a master of disguise and within minutes can duplicate the appearance of any other character by using facial putty. Plus, his tirades and hissy fits when his gang makes mistakes (which is often), calling them fools and idiots, are classic. And when the police raid his base of operations, he can immediately disguise himself as a doddering old man who has been tied up and beaten, pointing the finger of blame at hero Captain Midnight (who is a hero very much in the mold of Sky King, who uses airplanes and his skill as an aviator to capture the bad guys).

Of course Horne keeps his serials quirky, with Ivan Shark disguising himself as Captain Midnight himself, but his plans go awry when the police arrest him because they think Captain Midnight is a criminal. But soon he uses the confusion between identical Captain Midnights to his own advantage. Dave O'Brien is wonderful as the Captain, making his entirely black aviator costume and face mask with aviator goggles appear quite dashing. And whenever he is confronted by a challenge, he strikes a dramatic pose and momentary holds it, something straight out of silent cinema, but such dramatic flourishes work.

And the cliffhangers are grandiose and startling. In one sequence a plane drops a bomb straight down into the shack where Captain Midnight is hiding, and the building goes up in a puff of explosive smoke. In another sequence the Captain's plane is shot and it nose-dives into a field where it explodes on impact. In another chapter ending, Midnight is parachuting out of a plane when Ivan Shark, flying another plane, follows his descent and machine guns him as he drops to earth. But the finest torture finale is when Midnight is locked inside a chamber with a pole in the middle and the floor starts spinning around. Soon the walls of the chamber lift and we can see the spinning cylinder is atop a raging fire below, just waiting for the good Captain to be shaken loose. To help him fall, the metal lid to the pole slowly lowers, eventually forcing the Captain to either be crushed or let go and die in the fiery inferno below. This contraption is the very definition of what a good serial features.

Once again, *Captain Midnight* offers a fast pace, gripping story, a fine cast of characters and cliffhangers that elicit oooohs and ahhhhs. What more could a serial fan ever desire? And VCI, bless their hearts, features 15-chapter serials on two disks rather than printing one flip-over disc that could be easily scratched.

Jack Armstrong
Movie: 2.5; Disc: 3.0
[VCI Entertainment]

By 1947 the golden era of the American serial had passed, yet serials were still plenty of fun as this Columbia entry directed by Wallace Fox demonstrates. *Jack Armstrong*, based upon the popular radio series *Jack Armstrong, The*

All American Boy, stars the manly John Hart as Jack (Hart would replace Clayton Moore several years later as the Lone Ranger when a contract dispute put Moore out of the series for one season). Hart is obviously older than his teenage years require. Jack works with his uncle (Pierre Watkin) who looks definitely too old to be doing the derring-do activities required, but interestingly enough, with his leather jacket and floppy hat appears to be the model upon which Indiana Jones was based. The uncle's two children Billy (Joe Brown) and Betty (Rosemary La Planche, from *Strangler of the Swamp* and *Devil Bat's Daughter*) add little to the mix, especially the protected La Planche who sits out several action sequences.

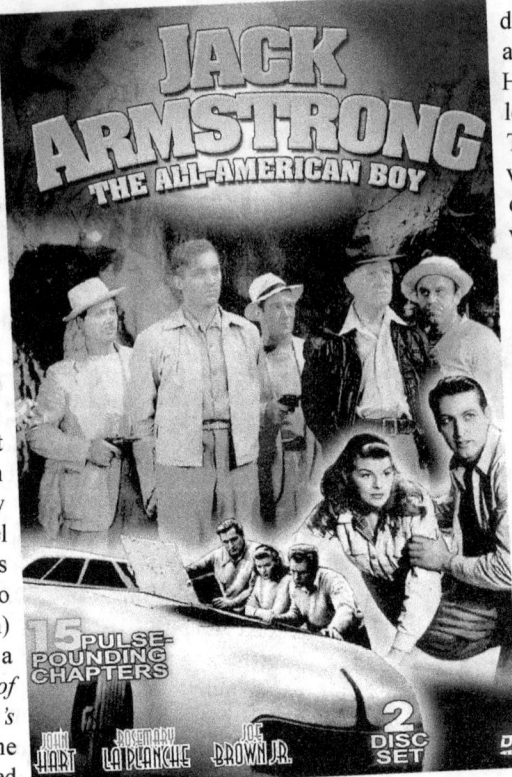

This 15-chapter serial stars an outstanding cast of serial regulars that always add interest to the mix. First of all, the magnificent Charles Middleton, not credited for some strange reason, plays the chief villain Jason Grood. Jack Ingram, the evil Green Archer from *The Green Archer*, plays Blair, the chief thug working for Grood. Eddie Parker, stunt man of Universal monsters fame (known mostly for playing the Frankenstein Monster in *Frankenstein Meets the Wolf Man* in more sequences than Bela Lugosi did), plays thug Slade who dies before the last chapter.

After an urban setting beginning, the serial rapidly moves to and remains on a desert island populated with the weirdest looking natives this side of Haight–Ashbury. Wearing gaudy plaids and checkered shirts and tunics, these natives look decidedly low rent. The leader of the opposition tribe who befriends Jack and crew is named Umala, who constantly is viewed running at break-neck speed back and forth with a shit-eating grin on his face. And the sexy leader of the tribe is Princess Alura (Claire James) who mistakenly believes that Grood's amplified voice is the voice of their tribal god.

The plot involves Grood's efforts to conquer the world with a super weapon mounted aboard a rocketship. Grood's men kidnap a scientist friend of Jack and his Uncle Fairfield, who is brought to the island but seems a little too willing to aid the madman's efforts (but secretly he is a government agent working for the good guys). Jack and the Fairfields follow him to the island to rescue him and prevent world domination.

The major flaw with *Jack Armstrong* is that the tone is juvenile and silly and sometimes even our serial believability is challenged. But director Wallace Fox keeps the action fast and furious and John Hart makes a generally emotionless but handsomely strong hero. Though it is Charles Middleton's villainy as Grood, his stern orders delivered in a quivering yet calm voice, that maintains interest.

Jack Armstrong is not the best serial VCI offers, but with its restored print and sharp density, it is definitely a serial to revisit and enjoy.

Mystic River
Movie: 3.0; Disc: 4.0
[Warner Bros.]

This past year *Mystic River* and *Lord of the Rings: The Return of the King* vied for honors (via the Academy Awards, critics top-10 lists; industry guilds, etc.) as best film of 2003. On the one hand we have the mega-budget splashy CGI-enhanced special effects bonanza, directed by relative newcomer Peter Jackson. In the other corner we have the lower-budgeted acting-dominated human drama, directed by aging icon Clint Eastwood.

I believe the Oscars got it right.

While *Mystic River* offers the same type of intense acting provid-

ed by the late Marlon Brando in such 1950s films as *On the Waterfront*, and while the cast is never less than superb (Sean Penn, Tim Robbins, Kevin Bacon, Marcia Gay Harden and Laura Linney), *Mystic River* for me is nothing better than a solid three-star movie.

First of all everyone states this is Sean Penn's movie, and while his performance as Jimmy reminds me of an early Brando performance, the character he creates is a punk. When his daughter is missing and perhaps murdered, Jimmy and his two thugs charge the policemen who are maintaining a perimeter. Screaming, his face ravished with anguish, he and his thugs appear to be mad dogs held in check by the overwhelming number of men in blue. Next we find out that Jimmy committed a robbery and did prison time, and afterwards, murdered a man who is the father of the boyfriend of his murdered daughter. Secretly, he has been sending the family $500 per month, making it seem that the father ran off but still supports his family.

Boyhood friend Dave (Robbins) comes home in the middle of the night (the same night that Jimmy's daughter is murdered) to an upset wife, his hands swollen and bloody, a knife slash wound across his abdomen. In tears the formerly sexually abused little boy claims he came across a car where a sexual predator was molesting a young boy in a parked car. Dave claims he lost it, he went off, and beat the predator to death. However, in the upcoming days, the newspaper fails to report such a "crime" ever occurred, and Dave's wife (Marcia Gay Harden) even begins to doubt the word of her husband, soon believing he killed Jimmy's daughter.

At the same time Jimmy hates his daughter's boyfriend and deaf-mute younger brother, but he does

Sean Penn won an Academy Award for his performance in *Mystic River*.

Mystic River belongs to Tim Robbins as the tortured molestation victim who becomes the victim of mob violence.

not know the boy is dating his daughter and the two planned to run off to Las Vegas to be married. The night of her violent murder she and her girlfriends celebrate by bar hopping and dancing seductively atop the neighborhood bar (in plain sight of an enamored Dave). However, the daughter suggests to her boyfriend that if her father found out about them, that her father would kill him.

By movie's end Jimmy, reverting to his thug nature, savagely murders Dave, first having his thug cronies get him drunk, and finally the posse takes him "out back" where Dave is forced to confess (Jimmy stating if he confesses to the truth, he will spare his life) but ends up with a knife in the belly and a slug in the brain, only hours before Kevin Bacon's cop apprehends the true murderer, Dave's story having been correct all along (the corpse of the child molester is finally found).

No matter how great a performance Sean Penn creates, the character of Jimmy is despicable, without salvation or redeeming qualities. How can we sympathize with a murderer who takes the law into his own hands?

For me the film belongs to Tim Robbins, the poor childhood victim of sexual molestation who is alienated by his childhood friends and psychologically flashes back the night of Jimmy's daughter's murder to lash out at the type of man who hurt him all those years ago. Dave, who desperately needs counseling and tender loving care, only receives doubt from his wife, and he cannot let anyone else know what he's done. And ultimately, Jimmy blames him for the murder of his daughter that he did not commit, but Dave blames himself for committing murder anyway (the sexual abuser he beat to death). Dave, as played by Tim Robbins, becomes the standout performance because he is holding so much inside and his taciturn face expresses so many demons being harbored there. It is a performance that is both subtle and virtuoso at the same time. Sean Penn, on the other hand, is all agony, pain and whining; unlike Dave, he is empty inside. So Penn's performance is all style with very little substance. Yes, Penn's performance is a *tour de force*, but the character is simply hollow and one-dimensional.

At well over two hours long, *Mystic River* is a superb character story of a working-class neighborhood and its history of internal demons, but that alone does not equal a great movie.

**The Judy Garland
Signature Collection
Meet Me in St. Louis: 3.5
Love Finds Andy Hardy: 3.0
In the Good
Old Summertime: 3.0
For Me and My Gal: 3.0
Ziegfeld Girl: 2.5
Disc: 4.0
[Warner Home Video]**

Warner Bros. remains at the forefront of restoring classic movies to their original radiance, and this recent release of a slew of Judy Garland movies more than proves the point. While perhaps only *Meet Me in St. Louis* is a bona fide classic, the other four movies are better-than-average entertainment and showcase Garland with other stars in various phrases of her movie career (*In the Good Old Summertime* near the end of her MGM career; *Love Finds Andy Hardy* one year before her star-making turn in *The Wizard of Oz*].

The gem of this collection is a remastered Dolby 5.1 surround (in "Ultra-Resolution" carefully restoring the original Technicolor negative) *Meet Me in St. Louis*, arguably among the top-three Garland classics ever made. This 1944 MGM film directed by Vincente Minnelli (soon to be her husband) attempts to create quaint nostalgia for the war-torn nation by reflecting upon a more optimistic world at the turn of the century, revolving around the 1904 World's Fair in St. Louis. Here is a world where Alonzo (Leon Ames) rules his family with a firm yet loving hand. Mother Anne (Mary Astor) frequently plays intermediary between stubborn, inflexible Alonzo and the children, especially the four daughters (Garland, Margaret O'Brien, Lucille Bremer and Joan Carroll). During an early sequence, Rose (Bremer) is expecting a telephone call from her beau who is away in college, and she desires some privacy expecting he very well may propose marriage. Alonzo insists that dinner be served at a specific time, but all the women in the household work in tandem to throw the schedule off by racing through dinner in a comedy of errors. These wily females who occupy the house easily manipulate Alonzo's rule of the roost. This extended family includes the live-in maid (Marjorie Main) and Grandpa (Harry Davenport). Under the external formality is revealed a loving, cohesive and supportive family underneath where everyone pitches in, thinking of the good of the family as a whole, rather than what's good for the individual. This concept is strained when

the father announces he has been promoted and forced to take a new job in New York, thus causing the family to pull up its roots, sever its social ties and move across the country. While Alonzo is excited over his new professional prospects, not even he appears too enthused over the move.

However, *Meet Me in St. Louis* is mainly remembered for Judy Garland's radiance and her wonderful rendition of classic songs such as "Meet Me in St. Louis," "The Trolley Song," "The Boy Next Door" and "Have Yourself a Merry Little Christmas" (a performance so dominant that this film is now known as a Christmas movie). Her rapport with the younger sister Tootie (Margaret O'Brien) forms the heart and soul of the movie. Tootie, the imaginative mischief-maker, is constantly concerned about the death and burial of her dolls and she is shattered over the thought of the future move to New York. In the film's pivotal sequence, Garland sings "Have Yourself A Merry Little Christmas" to Tootie, not as a festive, joyous celebration of the holidays, but as a tearful, emotionally painful reflection on time and change and the devastation that time can cause. It remains one of the most emotionally sorrowful sequences in movie history and demonstrates Garland's talents to melt the heart via her voice and song. While the Christmas sequence is so emotionally involving, the Halloween sequence, captured in dense Technicolor hues, is dark, moody and even terrifying, suggesting Val Lewton's *Curse of the Cat People* in color.

It is the Technicolor cinematography, set design, costuming and overall production detail that brings this turn-of-the-century Americana to stark life, each sequence appearing as vivid as postcards. Of course, after wringing our emotions for most of the movie, Alonzo finally decides that he will not uproot his family and instead remain in St. Louis, now pictured as the cosmopolitan center of the universe and exactly the place where his family belongs.

Extras on this two-disc platter include a wealth of entertainment. We have Liza Minnelli's introduction; commentaries by people including Margaret O'Brien and screenwriter Irvin Brecher; isolated music-only track; Vincent eMinnelli trailer gallery; documentaries on the making of the film and *Hollywood: The Dream Factory* and *Becoming Attractions: Judy Garland*. Also the pilot of a 1966 TV series based upon the movie is included, as is a short, *Bubbles*, featuring Judy Garland at age seven. Finally the Lux Radio Theater Broadcast, based upon the movie, is included.

Love Finds Andy Hardy (1938), the fourth and one of the best entries of the Andy Hardy series, introduces the character of Betsy Booth (Garland) as the girl next door. Judy Garland, portraying the typically perky teenager she probably desired to be, plays a more adult role than the one she played a year later as Dorothy in *The Wizard of Oz*. Surprisingly, Mickey Rooney never recognizes Garland for the beauty she was and constantly refers to her as a kid, his romantic eyes directed to regular girlfriend Polly (Ann Rutherford) and new beauty Cynthia (Lana Turner, in her first MGM film). No wonder Garland's self concept suffered, for as a beautiful teen, she was playing childish parts and was constantly referred to as a kid. Of course, when you perform alongside Lana Turner, most females come up short.

The plot, a typically devastating one for dorky Andy Hardy, involves him buying a car to take Polly to the holiday dance on Christmas Eve. He over-extends himself and buys a car, paying only part of the $25 sale price. He promises to pay the remaining $8 before the dance, but unfortunately finds Polly

Judy Garland, Margaret O'Brien & Tom Drake in *Meet Me in St. Louis*

will be away for the holiday. However a friend (fool that he is) pays Hardy to escort his date, Cynthia, to the dance, allowing the enterprising teen to buy his car. The movie's plot shows Rooney balancing the affections of these three women with Garland being the kid until she shows up at the dance wearing a beautiful and very adult-looking dress, finally attracting the eye of Andy Hardy. However, she politely puts him in his place, making sure he does the right thing by the other two women and all ends up well. Like *Meet Me in St. Louis*, *Love Finds Andy Hardy* recreates a more innocent America where small town life creates the ideal community that allows teenagers the flexibility of growing up and learning from their mistakes, which are never too serious. The rapport between the solemn (yet tender and loving) father Judge Hardy (Lewis Stone) and rascally son Andy becomes the emotional centerpiece, making the series one of the most popular in movie history.

Judy Garland and Gene Kelly in *For Me and My Gal*

The remaining Garland releases are all of interest. We have *In the Good Old Summertime* (1949), a remake of *The Shop Around the Corner*. Judy Garland and Van Johnson star as romantically inclined pen pals (their identities unknown to one another) who are antagonistic co-workers in their face-to-face relationship. While the original film is superior, the restructuring of the story as a musical is always of interest. *For Me and My Gal* (1942) directed by Busby Berkeley, introduced Gene Kelly in his film debut, finally falling in love with Garland by film's end after she joins his song-and-dance act in pre-WW1 vaudeville. However, the war calls and Kelly maims his hand to avoid the draft, causing Garland to leave him. But all works out well at the end. Finally we have *Ziegfeld Girl* (1941), a sprawling epic musical, that details the life of three Ziegfeld girls (Garland, Hedy Lamarr and Lana Turner), giving each girl a melodramatic back-story that is always told amid the world of dance and song. Judy Garland as Susan quits the vaudeville act run by her father to join the Ziegfeld Follies and create her new life of fame and fortune. Later on in the film, she has to help her father restore his floundering career.

For people who only know Judy Garland through her classic *The Wizard of Oz*, perhaps now is the time to investigate these diverse aspects of her movie career through these wonderful Warner Bros. DVD releases, crowned by a stellar release of the pivotal *Meet Me in St. Louis*.

www.ingramcontent.com/pod-product-compliance
Lightning Source LLC
Chambersburg PA
CBHW081728100526
44591CB00016B/2538